unintentionally
celibate

unintentionally celibate

by Olive B. Persimmon

Published by Dream Maiden Publishing

Copyright: © 2015 Olive B. Persimmon

Print ISBN-13: 978-0692376515

Print ISBN-10: 0692376518

Front cover photo: © J. L.

Front cover design: © David Weinstein

Back cover photo: © Katarina Kojic

Back cover design: © David Weinstein

Interior design and preparation for publishing:

Tony Loton of LOTONtech Limited (www.lotontech.com)

This is a work of creative nonfiction. The events are portrayed to the best of the author's memory. While all the stories in this book are true, some names and identifying details have been changed to protect the privacy of the people involved.

Printed in the United States of America

First Printing, 2015

Dedication

This book is for everyone who has ever done something ridiculous and was too embarrassed to talk about it. It's for everyone who has ever failed a job interview or sucked at dating. It's for everyone who is afraid to talk about sex because they think their number is too high or too low, or accidentally burned their boyfriend's penis with lotion like I did.

I hope this book makes you laugh. But I also hope it makes you not give a shit.

Prologue

(You really need to read this)

I'm twenty-seven and, as of writing this, I haven't had sex in two years, six months, three days, and two and a half hours. It's a situation that I wish upon no one. Over these two and a half years I've learned two facts.

Fact one: Granny panties never lead to coitus.

Fact two: Using the word *coitus* never leads to coitus.

Don't get me wrong, I like sex. A lot. Like, a lot a lot. I don't have any sort of traumatic history or body issue hang-ups. I'm not super religious or an advocate for abstinence.

I'm somehow Unintentionally Celibate.

My friends frequently ask me why I'm not doing the deed. "Ya, but you *could* be having sex," they state when I complain for the millionth time.

Yes. That is true. Because anyone with the right physical anatomy *could* be having sex. Plus I live in New York City, where anyone with a vagina can walk into a bar and leave with someone.

So what do I want?

Sexy, dirty sex with someone I trust and respect. Possibly a boyfriend.

See, here's the thing: I'm not really a casual-sex kind of girl.

Over these two years, six months, three days, and two and a half hours of celibacy, I've had several casual relationships. I've gone on an enormous number of first dates, second dates, even fifth dates.

But no Facebook-official, you're-totally-my-girlfriend relationships.

Throughout this time there's also been a lot of almost sex with these almost boyfriends.

1

Almost.

Plenty of orgasms but never full-on-insertion, thrusting-in-and-out, we're-doing-this-till-everyone-gets-off sex.

My friend Kate, who is getting her master's in psychology, offered her unsolicited opinion about my "situation."

"It's odd that you didn't have sex with any of the guys you were dating. If I had to guess, I'd say the root of the problem stems from your—"

I cut her off before she could finish her diagnosis. "First off, we were casually dating and second off, don't overanalyze it. Things ended before insertion. Simple as that."

But I guess it wasn't really as simple as that. My entrance into the world of sex (which you'll read about) wasn't as seamless as it could have been. Don't get me wrong, it wasn't terrible but it wasn't amazing either. Shortly after that, I moved to NYC where I was incapable of finding a good ol' relationship. It started out unintentionally, but after a year of no p-in-the-v it became a thing. I got stuck in a weird vortex of no sex.

"Ok. Ok. I'm just gonna say that at this point in the game, you need a slumpbuster to get you out of this rut. I know it's not your thing, but casual sex might be the solution here," Kate said.

Kate had never been in a sex famine so it was easy for her to prescribe a solution. In fact, she'd had a steady stream of boyfriends since the sixth grade. I, on the other hand, looked exactly like the female version of George Costanza when I was in sixth grade. Not only was I seriously overweight, I had nerdy glasses with giant rims, an unflattering haircut, and an enormous yellow Windbreaker that I wore on a daily basis. Middle school years are awkward for most people but I was definitely in the upper echelons of Uncool.

If all that wasn't bad enough, I insisted on dressing myself in monochromatic outfits. All my shirts had an animal performing an action on them. I had a pink sweater with penguins knitting to match my pink ribbed leggings. A hunter green shirt with dogs painting to match my XL green cotton shorts. A denim button-up with an embroidered horse jumping a fence to match my only pair of tight-at-the-ankles light denim jeans.

You get the picture.

While my wardrobe may have been acceptable in the fashion mayhem of the '80s, or for a four-year-old, I was twelve and it was 1998.

I've always thought my mom was pretty cool. So it blows my brain why she sent her kid to school in color-coordinated outfits with flowered granny panties (an underwear habit that wasn't broken until college).

Many years later, I asked my mom why she let me go out in public dressed like a Teletubby.

"You could have spared me years of teasing," I told her.

"You chose those outfits. You were unique," she said. "You wore whatever you wanted and you wouldn't let anyone tell you otherwise. In fact, you still do that. I tried to tell you the other day that your ugly smiley-face dress isn't the most flattering."

"No way. That dress is awesome," I argued. She gave me a see-my-point look.

Needless to say, my looks and clothing choices didn't make me the girl everyone wanted to date.

But I was oblivious to all this.

Until one day in gym.

It was dodgeball day.

The team captains had already chosen most of the athletic kids. There were only four people remaining, including myself, when Matt Corvington, my longtime crush, said, "I guess I'll take Costanza." It was the first time I'd heard I was nicknamed Costanza. Everyone laughed as my face turned bright red. I ambled over to my team's side, my head hung in shame.

Kids are assholes.

It was the start of my comedic tragedy and also the beginning of a life of hijinks. Life is funny for short, fat, balding men. Life is even funnier for twelve-year-old girls who look like short, fat, balding men. There are only two choices for fat kids: get smart or get funny. I got smunny. I became a nonconformist with a sharp tongue and a soft spot for the underdog.

Fast-forward to twenty-seven. I'm decently attractive and I don't look like George Costanza anymore. But I'm still not getting any. I'm not smelly, bitchy, crazy, or weird either. The only conclusion I can come to is that it might have something to do with the fact that I wear space pants to the grocery store and blog about all the sex I'm not having.

"Are you actually going to post that on the Internet?" my roommate asked.

"Ya, girl. I don't give a shit. It's important to write the truth, even if it makes you look bad." I laughed.

It was inevitable that I would grow up and write a book.

My life was meant to be full of illogical happenings, humorous situations, and neurotic behaviors. This book chronicles these tales. I regret to inform you that all the following stories are true depictions of real-life situations. Don't worry though, this isn't a pathetic, "I'm-eating-ice-cream-all-day-and-feeling-bad-for-myself" kind of book where I lament my love life or lack of sex. Yes, some of the stories are about coitus, but most aren't. It's partially a book about growing up as a fat kid and trying to get laid. Mostly though, it's just a book about shenanigans.

In any event, I hope it makes you laugh.

But if there's only one thing you'll get from this book, it's that granny panties won't get you laid. Ever.

PART 1: THE MAKING OF AN UNINTENTIONAL CELIBATE

Before there was celibacy, there was an awkward kid with dog shit on her pants and a fake sex blog

...and other stories that explain what kind of kid grows up to become **Unintentionally Celibate**.

The Incident

I just wanted to be a normal kid. But normalcy was meant for other people. Not for future Unintentional Celibates.

My only goal was to complete middle school without an emotionally scarring episode. I wanted to fly under the radar, unknown and undiscovered. As a fat kid, that was the only way to escape the teasing of my peers.

The universe had other plans.

It's unreasonable to think that a batch of lotion can "go bad." But that's exactly what I thought on the day of "The Incident." If I had been thinking a little more rationally, perhaps I would have realized the smell was the dog shit all over my leg.

As always, I was running late for school that day. After pressing snooze on my alarm too many times, I frantically jumped out of bed. I had ten minutes before the bus came. I threw on some clothes and flew out the door. As I sprinted wildly, my Windbreaker billowed behind me. I ran through my neighbor's backyard and arrived at the bus stop just in time to see the magical yellow glow one house away. The bus came and I entered, sweating and panting heavily.

Struggling to catch my breath, and straightening my glasses, I took my normal seat.

There was an obvious hierarchy on the bus in regard to seating. The cool kids sat in the back, the almost-cool kids in the middle, and me dead in the front. I couldn't figure out why my tremendous talent in classical theater roles and my affinity for the children's show *Zoom* didn't push me into middle school stardom. And I hate to brag, but the hottest boy in school did ask me out on a date...and although he was joking...and although his friends laughed about it rather loudly at lunch...it still counted, damn it! In my mind, I was backseat material. In everyone else's minds, I didn't belong on the bus at all.

A few stops later, my almost-cool-but-not-cool-enough-to-sit-in-the-middle friend Christa sat across from me. She pulled out her new Bath & Body Works lotion. In those days, lotion and body-spray products were like crack in East Cleveland. Everyone had some; everyone wanted more. The only acceptable gift for any girl's birthday was more scented lotion or body spray, and it certainly couldn't be an off brand.

Christa pulled out a brand-new bottle of Vanilla Breeze lotion and generously offered me some. I took a large portion and coated my hands and neck.

"Dang, Christa. This new scent smells great," I said.

We quickly moved on to other subjects and pulled out our homework before arriving at school. While struggling with a division worksheet, we noticed an offensive odor wafting up toward our noses.

"Oh my God. What is that smell?" Christa said.

"Dang. It's terrible!" I said, scrunching up my nose.

We complained for another three minutes before deciding to investigate. After a minute of contemplation, I came to the only conclusion I could think of. "I think it's your lotion. You must have gotten a bad batch."

Horror struck Christa's face. It was the worst thing that could happen to anyone in middle school.

"OHMYGOD Are we gonna smell like this all day?" Christa cried, her dreams of preppy popularity slipping between the cracks.

"I dunno, but if I were you, I would throw away that lotion."

We both exited the bus, attempting to cover the smell with other body lotion. We borrowed three different kinds from other girls but nothing made it disappear. We entered school together, met our friend Billy, and sat at a lunch table in the cafeteria before the first bell rang.

After a minute, with the typical tact of a seventh-grade male, Billy said, "What smells like shit?"

Embarrassed, Christa clammed up. I waited for her response and when it didn't come, I stated very matter-of-factly, "Christa got a bad batch of lotion. It goes sour after it touches your skin. We both used it."

"Gross," he said, plugging his nose dramatically as the bell rang.

In the hallway on the way to my first class, I heard two popular eighth-graders comment about the odor.

"Why does this school always smell so fucking bad?"

"Ya, man. It smells like farts."

I turned tomato red. I cursed Bath & Body Works, cursed Christa, and cursed the Good Lord himself for getting me into this situation.

I finally made it to first-period geography where I sat in front of my friend Tim. I opened my pencil case and pulled out my packet of colored pencils. Today we were coloring a map of Argentina. My geography teacher was super weird. He was really into coloring maps and was literally obsessed with Alec Baldwin. He had a signed napkin from Alec framed on his desk and a taxidermy cat who had been named Baldwin. After someone complained that he had no pictures of female role models in the room, he hung a picture of Sacajawea. "We can all learn from Sacajawea," he said.

He loved the Milton Bradley game "Cootie." He always picked his favorite students to play. Nobody liked to be picked.

Tim and I were exchanging green colored pencils of different shades when he said, "Man, it smells like cheese in here."

11

I looked around, making sure no one else was listening, and replied hastily, trying to downplay the situation. "Oh, it's just my friend's bad lotion that I used this morning."

Tim scrunched up his face.

"That doesn't make any sense. Why would lotion smell like cheese?"

I sent him a nasty look and said defensively, "It was a bad batch. It spoiled or something and now it smells. It goes sour when it touches skin. I don't know. Maybe someone got the mixture wrong, Tim!"

My aggressive whispering finally drew the attention of our creepy teacher.

"Olive and Tim, Argentina must look pretty blank with the amount of talking you're doing. Silence is golden; let's get rich," he said in his monotone voice.

Tim waited a few minutes before whispering back. He couldn't leave it alone. "No. It really smells like rotting, molding, disgusting cheese. I've never smelled anything so bad in my whole life."

"Yeah, Tim. I already told you, the lotion went bad. LET IT GO," I said, furiously coloring the borders.

Then, in the next fifteen seconds, "The Incident" came to a head. Tim slowly looked down at the floor by my desk. His face began to change, with a span of emotions. It went from confusion to understanding, and then to laughter. He grinned before saying the terrifying words that would chill any middle-schooler:

"Um, I'm pretty sure the cheese smell is coming from the dog shit all over your leg."

I looked down. Dog shit was splattered up the back and side of my left jean leg.

I panicked.

Middle-schoolers are the worst people on the planet. If anyone found out about this, I was done.

I knew I needed to go to the bathroom to clean it but if I left in the middle of class I would draw attention to myself. I looked at the clock. We still had fifteen minutes till the end of the period. I agonized about what to do. "Wait it out. Go now. Wait it out. Go now." Time passed with infinite slowness. Minutes felt like hours as it was now glaringly obvious that there was dog shit all over my leg.

"I'LL KILL YOU IF YOU SAY ANYTHING!" I frantically scribbled on a note to Tim in green colored pencil.

Finally the bell rang. I bolted to the bathroom. I grabbed a wad of wet paper towels and ran into a stall to clean my leg. After ten minutes, I successfully got it off, leaving a giant wet spot where the poop had been. I breathed a sigh of relief. Tim was the only person who knew my secret.

The bell rang while I was still in the bathroom, so I was late to my second-period art class. By the time I arrived, the class was already working on magazine collages. We were creating artistic vision boards of what we wanted our future lives to be like. I tried to enter discreetly and take my seat by the window. While everyone was busy cutting out pictures of hot models, I quietly ripped out some perfume samples. I started rubbing them down my leg.

I smiled, relieved. I was going to get away with it.

Until Tim came over.

The little son of a bitch.

"Why are you rubbing perfume samples all over your leg?"

I flashed him a look of fury and indignation.

"Must be to cover up the dog-poop smell!" he said, bent over with laughter.

I looked around to see if anyone had heard.

The closest person, Michelle Altieri, was too engrossed in her search for the perfect magazine husband.

Tim saw me glance toward Michelle. He understood what was at stake here. We were friends. He didn't want me to fall any lower on the popularity scale.

He stopped bringing it up openly. But he was a middle school boy, which meant he couldn't let it go either. Instead, he spent the rest of art class bringing me additional perfume samples, laughing every time he dropped one on my desk.

****

I lost contact with Tim after high school. We didn't speak for years until, at the age of twenty-five, I moved to New York City, where Tim was a professional musician. We reconnected one night at a bar close to my apartment. After a few hours of childhood reminiscing and nostalgia, I turned to him and said, "You know, you were present for one of the most embarrassing moments of my life."

"What are you talking about?" He looked confused.

"When I had dog shit all over my leg and you kept bringing it up in art class."

"I don't remember that at all. Why did you have shit on your leg?" Tim asked sincerely, sipping a beer.

"You don't remember? In the seventh grade?" I said.

"I have no idea what you're talking about."

I reminded him of the story and he laughed as hard as he had the first time. Enough time had passed that I was able to laugh about it too. I had come a long way since middle school.

I was surprised that he didn't remember but I guess that's a pretty good life lesson. In middle school, a leg full of shit is the end of the world. But that kind of stuff only lives on in the hearts and minds of traumatized nerds everywhere.

I'm even considering joining a dodgeball team.

Preggo

The first time someone asked me if I was pregnant, I was twelve and enjoying some fried cheese at the Summit County Fair. That was the first time out of nine that someone has called me pregnant. I've been pregnant never.

I thought every civilized member of society knew that you never, and I mean NEVER, ask a woman any question that is remotely related to the word *pregnant*. Even if you suspect it, don't whisper, infer, imply, ask, insinuate, or congratulate. EVER. Women are perfectly aware of any spare-tire, muffin-top bulge they may have. The last thing we need is a stranger reminding us that they're aware of it too. Personally, I'd prefer to live in the delusion that everyone else thinks I look fabulous and wants to have sex with me. No one wants to have sex with a pregnant lady.[1]

I didn't always look pregnant. In fact, I was a pretty cute baby. Sweet dimples, nice smile. A cute toddler too. I was equipped with the genetic potential to become a decent hottie. Unfortunately, at the tender age of eleven, I started a diet of twenty-five freeze pops a day. Freeze pops consist of three basic ingredients: water, sugar, and highly processed food coloring (every child's dream of a culinary delicacy). When my mom first noticed that I was gaining weight, she tried to enforce moderation with a two-desserts-a-day rule—one after lunch and one after dinner. Freezies counted. But they were grab and go. It was too easy to sneak one from the freezer, bite off the top with my teeth, and slurp it down before anyone caught me. Soon after, I was an addict. I was chain-consuming one after another and stashing the plastic wraps in the bottom of the trash bin below the coffee grinds. I was perpetually on a sugar high and running around like Rambo. Thanks to my frozen-food habit, over the course of one year I gained thirty

---

[1] Except for some people who actually DO want to have sex with a pregnant woman. Like my former friend with benefits. But that's a story for a different chapter.

pounds and became the pregnant-looking version of Attila the Hun.

The first person who insisted I was pregnant was a girl with visibly bad hygiene and a full-time job as the operator of a traveling fun house.

I was at the fair with my best friend at the time, Erika. Erika and I had a crafting business back in those days. We made homemade candles, pens, and beaded jewelry that we sold from a table in Erika's front yard. Beyond our families, we only ever had one customer. She lived on our block and always took vigorous evening walks around the neighborhood. On the day of the fair, she stopped by our table and ordered a ten-dollar candle. She paid in full. We promised to hand-deliver it to her home upon completion. Unfortunately for her, Erika and I weren't good businesswomen. That night, we spent her ten dollars on entertainment and cotton candy at the fair; we delivered her candle a year later by ding-dong ditching it on her doorstep.

The county fair was the same as always. Raunchy smells and rides run by men named "Crazy Larry." When you're twelve, the county fair is a pretty big deal. It's a breeding ground for young hormones and budding relationships. It was the only place I could go and expect to see my newest crush, Tommy Hoover. There was a good chance too that he would be there, because *everyone was there.* Tommy went hoping that his crush, Jamie Simpson, was there. But I pretended that Jamie Simpson didn't exist and put on my best matching outfit to strut my stuff.

The county fair was like being at an outdoor Wal-Mart with rides. Every few feet there was a sick-looking kid who had just vomited. His grossly overweight parent was eating chocolate-covered fries with bacon. There were lots of mullets. A lot of bad odors. Three or four guys walked around in pit-stained 'beaters, carrying a giant stuffed tiger. I also saw a lot of disturbing things, like old women in sequined belly-shirts and cowboy hats. Dirty men being mean to their kids. That sort of stuff.

There was a "Freak Show" claiming to host some of the world's finest oddities. I paid four dollars to enter, expecting to be amazed by the exhibits inside. What I found instead was a miniature pony and a midget lady. I looked at the woman for a second and quickly came to the conclusion that she wasn't an oddity at all. In fact, she was quite beautiful.

"Hi. I'm Olive. What's your name?"

"Paula."

She sounded bored.

"It's nice to meet you, Paula," I said.

She frowned slightly and abruptly nodded her head in my direction. I could tell she didn't want to have a conversation with me and suddenly I was really sad. I was sad because there was Paula, beautiful and small, sitting around in a cheap polyester dress at the county fair, where people paid four dollars to stare at her.

Something about it didn't seem right. To this day, I still think that's a little fucked-up.

I smiled weakly at Paula one last time and pushed the curtain back to leave. My eyes watered as social consciousness began to kill my buzz. I had always been an oversensitive child. Noticing that the energy had changed, Erika immediately went into full best-friend mode. She offered me some cotton candy and suggested we prowl around to find Tommy. I balked at both of these suggestions, so she decided to play the big card. It was the bona fide cure for sadness: the fun house.

I reluctantly agreed.

After waiting in line, we handed our tickets to a mean-looking carnie. Her hair was greasy and matted in a ponytail. She was missing a tooth. She looked at our tickets, looked at me, and scowled.

Her lip turned up and she growled, "Pregnant women aren't allowed on this ride, ma'am."

I looked around to find the person she was talking to. I searched the line before returning to her persistent stare. After a painfully awkward minute, I realized she was talking to me. My face flushed with shame and embarrassment. Too shocked and stupefied to respond, I stood there with my mouth hanging open. Luckily Eri, always the badass, stepped in quickly.

"She's twelve, lady. She's not pregnant!"

A moment of silence passed. The carnie scrunched up her forehead. I could see the wheels churning in her brain. She considered Erika's words and said, "Look, it's for your health, ma'am, and for the health of the *baby*. You're not allowed on the ride."

I stared at her in disbelief. I was wearing a shirt with cartoon kittens on it and didn't look a day older than twelve...a fat twelve-year-old, but twelve nonetheless. In the same way Eri was a badass, I was painfully shy. I stared at the ground for a while until I finally found my voice and said, "I'm really not pregnant."

"Fine," she replied, throwing the word out with a mixture of repulsion and anger.

It wasn't over yet though. Carnies can't let things go. They need the last word. As I entered the fun house, she looked at me in disgust and spat her final jab.

"I know you're lying."

Now, it's an extremely tactless and rude thing to ask a woman if she's pregnant. But it's a totally different carnie level of rude to *insist*.

Needless to say, the fun house was no longer fun. We walked through the rest of it halfheartedly. As we exited, I was mortified and ready to leave, even though I still hadn't seen Tommy Hoover.

That was the last year I went to the Summit County Fair. To this day, I still feel an inherent dislike for carnies.

Up until that point, I hadn't fully realized how fat I had gotten. However, after being attacked by a complete stranger, on top of my new dodgeball nickname, I could no longer remain in denial. The reality hit me hard. I needed to make a change.

That moment at the fair was the catalyst for my entrance into the world of roundhouse kicks. Erika's mom loaned me her Billy Blanks Tae Bo VHS tape.[2] I punched, kicked, and uppercut my way to a slimmer body and managed to lose thirty pounds before the next school year started. On the first day back at school, I was feeling confident. Boys checked me out. My friends didn't recognize me.

I thought that would be the end of my pregnancy woes. But it wasn't. Despite busting my butt to lose my jiggle, eight more people would insinuate that I was pregnant.

The second time occurred several years later. I was sixteen years old and working at Jo-Ann Fabrics. I had lost a lot of weight and Erika's badassery had finally rubbed off a little. I won't say I was cool, because I wasn't. But I was better equipped to deal with the next pregnancy implication. I was lifting a heavy bolt of fabric when a customer politely said, "Honey, I can carry that if you're expecting." I chuckled a little and told her kindly that I wasn't.

---

[2] Mrs. Hunt, if you're reading this, I'm sorry I never returned it.

Unlike the carnie, she seemed adequately embarrassed and apologized profusely.

The third and fourth insinuations aren't really that notable except to acknowledge that I was getting some pretty thick skin.

I'm not really sure why everyone thought I was pregnant. The only conclusion I can come to is that I've been cursed with an odd body shape. I'm a short girl with large breasts, a nonexistent butt, and slim legs and arms. The only place I carry fat is a little pouch in my stomach.

By the fifth implication, I was able to handle it. I was twenty-two and at a training to become an AmeriCorps volunteer. I was attempting to fulfill postgraduate idealism before entering the corporate cog machine. The kind of people you meet at a training to be an AmeriCorps volunteer are granola-eating, idealist hippies.

But the one who called me preggo wasn't that kind.

She was a large, older woman in cutoffs. Her stomach was being oppressed by her jeans and waging a war to escape. She was probably thirty-five but looked like she was going on fifty-two.

I opened the door of my room at the hotel when I heard her holler down the hall, "YOU GOT A LIGHTA?"

She looked me up and down and, before I could even move my mouth to respond, she smirked. "Nah, YOU ain't got no lighta."

She examined me again. Her eyes stopped and focused on my belly. Suddenly her face lit up with excitement as she exclaimed, "OH, GIRL! You pregnant?"

I flushed, as always, but then chuckled, as the second, third, and fourth times had taught me to do. I responded that I wasn't.

She looked adequately disappointed and said, "You sure, girl? Oh well, gotta go find me a lighta."

I looked at her in utter disbelief. Of course I was sure.

The sixth, seventh, and eighth times happened at my first job out of college. Ironically, I worked in human resources. I thought that sort of thing would be taboo.

Wrong again.

The craziest thing was that my coworkers were well-educated, considerate people. How could civilized members of society not know any better than to ask about pregnancy? I can only conclude that they must have been pretty fucking sure.

The ninth and final time occurred just after I had moved to New York City. I was probably in the best shape of my life.

I was at dinner with my friend Cici and her temporary roommate, Sam. He was temporary because he was apartment searching; though, eight weeks later when he still didn't have an apartment, we questioned how hard he was actually searching. That kind of stuff happens in New York if you're not careful. Suddenly your roommate's cousin who is "for sure going to make it so big someday" can't afford his apartment. He'll wind up crashing with you till he gets back on his feet, which will be never, as long as he can continue mooching your food and toilet paper. Over tacos, I told Cici and Sam about my plight of always being called pregnant.

Sam gawked. "No way! You don't look remotely pregnant. You're making this up."

Make it up? Really? I can't come up with one legitimate reason why anyone would make up stories about being called pregnant.

Sam didn't believe me. He brought it up several times for the next few months. Until one time he said, out of the blue and with much authority, "It must be that you're always wearing those baggy Asian shirts."

I'm not sure what he was talking about, but he seemed certain.

As if the universe were conspiring to prove the validity of my story, the ninth time happened in front of Sam. We were in a subway station, waiting for the train from Brooklyn to Manhattan. A man in tattered sweatpants approached me. He wasn't wearing any shoes.

"Have any spare change?" he asked.

I pulled out a dollar and handed it to him.

"Thanks," he said.

"The sun is so bright. Elephants sing. I'm gonna buy a coffee with this dollar. BUT they're watching," he muttered in my direction.

The number one rule in New York is to never engage crazy people in conversation.

I'm not very good at this rule. I'm afraid that if I don't, they'll get mad and then really go crazy. Also, I'm from Ohio, which means it's ingrained in my blood to be polite, even to people who don't deserve it.

"Hmmm," I replied to his muttering.

That was enough permission for him to start chatting. He started telling jokes and laughed a lot. I laughed a lot too, though I'm not sure about what. I figured it was probably better to laugh every time he said something he found funny. When the train arrived, he followed me, still rambling.

As we entered the train, he turned and looked me squarely in the face. "I can see it in your face. You ain't no liar," he said.

I laughed and responded, "I've never been very good at lying."

"Other people maybe, but not you. You ain't got no lying bone in you at all." He turned abruptly toward a handsome man who was sitting down.

Without warning, he said, "Sir, would you mind getting up for my friend here? She's pregnant."

Sam's eyes popped open in shock. I blushed and threw my hands up in the air.

"I told you," I said to Sam.

The handsome man turned toward me and, in the cutest British accent, said, "I'm so sorry, ma'am. I didn't realize you were pregnant or I would have gotten up."

Of course he had to be a British dreamboat.

I blushed deeper. "Oh. I'm not."

He looked confused and I reiterated, "I'm not pregnant."

He looked at the man, and then back at me. He was perplexed. Then he handled the situation in a way that only a hot British dreamboat can. He made a cute joke and offered me his seat anyway. I declined awkwardly. We chatted for a few minutes until he got off the train, winking at me on the way out.

Sam turned and said, "Oh. My. God! I can't believe I experienced that firsthand. Wow. And you're not even wearing a baggy Asian shirt."

Every time I tell someone that nine people have insinuated that I was pregnant, that person tries to rationalize on my behalf. They say things like, "Obviously those people are insane." Or "It must be because you have a natural glow."

And I wish I could believe them.

But, at some point in time, I had to be honest with myself. Nine times is too many times to be that naïve. Think of it this way: The first time someone asks you if you're pregnant, you've met an asshole. The second time, you're unlucky with the amount of assholes you've met. But three times?

After three times—no doubt about it, it's you. And you look pregnant.

A/S/L, Wanna Cyber?

"Age/Sex/Location, wanna cyber?" I typed slowly in the chat room for "Horny, Single People." It was a universal phrase known by kids everywhere in the mid-nineties. I pressed Enter. My screen filled with a barrage of private messages.

I was thirteen when I became sexually cyber active. On a typical weeknight, I'd spend my evenings volunteering at a local nursing home. After reading mail to Ethel and painting Pearl's nails, I'd return home and log on to the Internet to get down and dirty with Bigpimp221 or Hugedick696. I was acting like a desperate fifty-four-year-old male.

I was perusing the Internet for online relationships, porn, and sexy chat rooms.

Up till this point, my sexual knowledge was based on trashy romance novels and *90210* episodes. Like any kid, I was curious. My understanding of the human anatomy was ill-informed and incomplete. I was young (and still coming out of my fat phase), so I could hardly explore my curiosity with any living human being. I turned to the Internet for information. Before Napster was illegal, I was carefully typing "pornography" into the video search and waiting an hour for Bangbus to load. Unfortunately, Bangbus usually involved a woman being treated like a disposable object. Even at a young age, my feminist side felt uncomfortable with this. I think some of this early porn watching colored my views on casual sex. I knew I never wanted to be treated like I was disposable.

Despite my attempts to educate myself about human sexuality, my Internet research was insufficient. Case in point: I still believed hair went all the way up the penis "Chewbacca-style" until I was a sophomore in high school. Although I occasionally watched porn, my preferred Internet activity was online chatting. For anyone seeking an education, online chat rooms are not the best place to go for knowledge advancement.

After a few months on the Internet, I found my first boyfriend. He was hot, romantic, and generally a catch. I knew this because his screen name, HotRomantiGuy347, told me so. I met him in an online chat room where "SeXXXy Men Meet SeXXXy Women."

Our relationship started like most online relationships.

"Hey Baby. A/S/L, Wanna Cyber?" he asked.

He called me baby; I swooned.

"18/Female/California," I responded.

I wasn't anywhere close to eighteen and I lived in Ohio. I was catfishing before catfishing was a thing.

I told him I lived in California because I'm a paranoid person.

I blame my father.

When I was young, my dad told me if anyone ever rang the doorbell, I should "hide under the bed until they go away." It didn't matter if it was a Girl Scout or a Jehovah's Witness; they were out to get me. To this day, I still put a piece of tape over my webcam in case anyone tries to hack it. This paranoia made me a blatant online liar. My boyfriend never had any chance of finding me. Everything he knew about me was exactly what I wasn't: tall, blond, thin, a dancer, eighteen, green-eyed. My name was Jade (because when you're thirteen, everyone wants to be named Jade or something else insanely dumb). I don't remember what his name was, but it was probably Caden or Luke or whatever the male equivalent of Jade is.

I learned a lot about love that year.

Like it can't exist in your parents' house, on the family computer. Because, God forbid your father walks in and reads "OOOOooOOO. That feels good." on the chat room private IM. I was sly though, and managed to have an online relationship for a year and a half. [3]

Occasionally HotRomantiGuy347 and I had real conversations. I knew his favorite food was pizza and that he played soccer. He knew that my dream was to become a professional dancer (it wasn't) and that I loved bunnies (I didn't).

Mostly though, our conversations consisted of "What are you wearing?"

I only had two answers to this question: "nothing" and "a red, lacy thong." I didn't know what a thong was, but I had seen this question answered many times in the chat rooms.

The summer after I turned fourteen, I miraculously managed to snag my first non-Internet, real-life boyfriend, Alan. I put his picture in the front of my wallet. I prominently displayed that picture to friends and strangers while loudly announcing, "Oh this pic? It's just my BOYFRIEND." I met Alan through a friend and we had only hung out a few times. But in my mind I was off the market. I logged on to Yahoo chat to break the news to HotRomantiGuy347:

TinyDancer610: Hey, I have something I have to tell you ...

HotRomantiGuy347: Wat r u wearing??

TinyDancer610: Ur a really great guy and there's no easy way 2 say this...

TinyDancer610: but I have a boyfriend now so I think we have to end this

TinyDancer610: I hope you're not mad at me, it was unexpected

HotRomantiGuy347: ok

TinyDancer610: I'm so sorry! U r the best Boyfriend I ever had!

TinyDancer610: I hope we can stay friends!

---

[3] Dad, forgive me if you're reading this. Also, do me a favor and never bring this up.

HotRomantiGuy347 never responded. His final "ok" was the end of our cyber romance.

I might have been cyber-heartbroken if I didn't have Alan. Unfortunately, like most high school summer romances, our relationship was short-lived. By the second month of school, Alan had moved on.

I removed his picture from my wallet.

Single and alone, I once again turned to the Internet for love. I was too afraid and insecure to talk to actual boys at my school. The Internet was a safe place to be flirtatious without worrying about rejection. It was a place that satiated horniness without fear. I could say anything I wanted and I never needed to act on it.

This time however, I was tired of cybering. I was tired of cycling through the exact same conversations. I wanted something more imaginative and creative. I turned to the blogging world instead.

This was the era when the blogging site Xanga was all the rage. It was perfectly normal to unload teenage garbage on to the World Wide Web. Everyone I knew was writing every insecurity, crush, and petty fight online for the rest of the teenage population to view. My blog was a bit different. It was not a real representation of my life. In fact, it was 100 percent totally made-up.

Not only was it fictional, it was a sex blog.

In my fake, exciting life, I was Heidi, Sex Goddess, worshipped by men and women alike. I was a redhead and I had followers. The best thing about blogging was the followers. They were strangers who found my fake life so interesting that they wanted an update every time they logged on. The only catch was they didn't know it was my fake life. I think some of them lived vicariously through my soft-core porn blog, which is absurd because I had no idea, anatomically speaking, how the body functioned at all. (Actually, I'm still not sure I do.)

So now, real excerpts from my old sex blog, created under the name Jaded324 (of course):

Thursday, May 09, 2002

First entry. Don't know where the hell to begin, not that anyone gives a damn anyway. I'm just another messed-up person in this big carnival-like blog game. Doesn't bother me at all though. :) This journal is for me and no one else. I guess this is my disclaimer.

This is blatantly false. I needed an outlet for my imagination. In that sense, I was writing for me. But mostly, I was writing for everyone else. I was a glutton for attention and loved having fans. Every time someone liked or commented on a story, I felt a rush of excitement. My entire existence was validated by total strangers commenting on my latest works.

I had sex with Brian again this weekend. He makes me feel so good and when our bodies connect I feel a kind of amazing pleasure that is undescrible [sic]. I am not a slut! I have been dating Brian for about two months. I really do love him. The first time we fucked...made love...that sounds better, more like the beautiful act it was instead of the title of a whorehouse. God, I remember it well. He slowly undressed me and started kissing me, it so was romantic! He was incredibly gentle. Brian is more experienced than me, he has been around the block a few times. But he's not gross or anything. It's a good thing because he knows how to shift and move my body with his. I went over to his dorm this weekend and he was lying on his bed, naked. He was listening to Eminem and rubbing lotion on his body. He looked so seductive. I stripped off all my clothes and crept into bed with him. We made love for the rest of the night.

At this point in time, I was a freshman in high school. I didn't have the faintest inkling what college was like at all, proven by the fact that my boyfriend was rubbing lotion all over his body while listening to Eminem.

Wednesday, June 12, 2002

Wow...long time no see. Hmm not much has happened. I saw Brian a lot yesterday. He came over and he gave me this beautiful little snow globe. On the inside was the most beautiful figurine of a dancer. We sat around on the couch and talked for a few hours about our hopes and dreams until I started getting pretty darn horny. He was unsuspecting as my hand found its way down his pants. I started rubbing his penis through his clothes. He reacted to me and we started kissing. He grabbed my boob through my shirt. He knows just how to please me. My boobs are my favorite thing to be touched. Some people are leg or ear or vagina people but I am a boob person. I feel really sorry for anyone who doesn't have a guy who knows how to please them.

Alright, I know...I know...enough talk about boobs and nipples and so on.[4]

Sorry, I get carried away. It's just when I start thinking about it in detail I start typing and it makes me horny and I forget what I type. Damn, thinking about that makes me so horny. It's too late to call Brian. I don't want to wake my angel. Alright please excuse me while I "release my energies." lol...oh don't be too grossed out, tons of girls masturbate. I am only open because you don't know me and will probably never meet me. Alright be back in a few minutes. Alright, I am back...sorry about that ;)

Things were going too well. I needed to add more drama. My fans loved drama and pleasing the fans was important. So right when everything in my fake cyber love life seemed perfect, right before we would have bought a fake Internet house with a fake white fence, right before we had two fake cyber kids, everything went terribly sour.

---

[4] While reading these posts as an adult, I'm particularly disturbed by my overuse of the ellipsis.

Wednesday, June 19, 2002

I hate Brian. I have never felt so much dislike and disgust ever. I hate him with all my heart. I can't believe I ever loved him.

Wake up, love doesn't exist.

No...that's not true.

Love exists. Just not for me.

In my fake broken heart, I used my imagination to weave a tale of deceit. It involved cheating and the words "his cum was all over her face."

Sunday, July 07, 2002

Brian cheated on me.

I went over to his place to surprise him and cook him dinner. I thought we could have a nice peaceful evening at home so I picked up a movie too. I walked in because it's never locked and there he was.

On the couch. With some blond girl.

His pants were down and his cock was full and beautiful. His cum was dripping off her face. I could see it on her lips. I just stood there in horror. He pulled his pants up and jumped off the couch but you could still see his erection. He kept saying, "It's not what you think, forgive me..." But I couldn't hear the rest. I looked at her and she just sat there with this big, stupid grin. She had tasted him. She had what was mine.

She just sat there and looked at me, didn't even try to cover up. Brian tried to take my hand and I just turned around and started running. I threw the grocery bag onto the sidewalk and ran home. I kept running with those images stuck in my head. I stopped and vomited into a bush. I went home and cried for hours. Brian called but I hung up and I disconnected the phone.

How could he do that to me??!?!?!? How could he cheat on me?!?!? I will NEVER forgive him.

I was a total faker. My life was void of any drama so I needed to make up something exciting.

Anyone reading that post with a clear understanding of the how the male body worked would have questioned some of those statements. One reader commented, "He had just cum but he was still hard? Must be a superhuman man." Other men chimed in.

That was the climax of my fake love life. The end followed shortly thereafter. Readers started to question my credibility.

In the few days following, Brian tried to get back together. By then I was already dating an older man, Rick. According to my blog, he was "way awesomer than Brian ever was." I tried to recover from my snafu with Brian by writing about my sexual exploits with Rick. Readers loved the graphic posts.

It all came crashing to a halt when I accidentally called Rick by the wrong name several times throughout a new post. Some of my followers called me out on the discrepancy and asked curiously, "What the fuck happened to Rick?" I tried to cover it up but they were onto me. Two huge errors in one week.

The more I tried to backtrack, the more they questioned my validity. People started unsubscribing. I desperately tried to win them back with racy posts but they were gone for good. I was left alone and fan-less. No one was liking or commenting on my posts. It seemed useless to keep writing. That was the end of my exciting, fake sex life.

That should have put the kibosh on my Internet sex habits.

And it did. For a while.

Until I turned twenty-two. I had long been absent from the Internet sex scene. Unlike my childhood self, I had an active social life and was too busy for Internet hobbies.

At a party, a friend mentioned a new website called Second Life. He described it as a virtual game, like *The Sims*, where it was possible to create avatars. I was intrigued.

My fascination with online sex was strange. I didn't fit the mold of a creepy, antisocial Internet troll. I went on dates often and fooled around with guys.

But I was interested in Second Life.

Maybe it was my inexperience with actual sex. Perhaps it was the ability to remain faceless. Maybe I just wanted to get my jollies off and masturbate in my room before class and the Internet provided the necessary stimulation. It was a safe and STD-free way to explore horniness. Curious, and maybe feeling nostalgic, I logged on to Second Life later that night.

I created a sexy character named Liliana Dsouza. She was wearing a red thong. In Second Life, you could choose your destination. I clicked on "Pleasure Island." There were two other avatars there, one male and one female.

I ambled over to the male and typed "Hello" into the chat box.

"F8?" he asked.

I looked to the right side of the screen, where the directions were highlighted for newbies like me.

F8 meant to thrust forward or engage in sex. F7 to moan loudly. F6 to display extreme excitement. F6 F8 F7 F8 F7, I pressed in rapid succession while he was F8ing my avatar back.

I started laughing. The movements were odd and robotic. It wasn't stimulating or fun. I was bored.

I pressed F9 to orgasm, so I could log off and get on with my real life.

"Did you like that?" the male avatar asked.

"Sure. Bye," Liliana Dsouza replied.

Second Life pretty much marked the end of an era for me. My interactive affair with the Internet came to a halt. I was done cybering, chatting, and exploring avatars.

It's much easier to just watch porn.

Our Changing Bodies

(And Other Good Books I Should've Read)

Puberty. It turns sweet children into hormone-filled nutjobs. I was no exception.

Weird things start happening when teenagers hit puberty. Sixth-grade boys start having wet dreams and explicit fantasies about their teachers. They start having unexpected erections while reading *The Giver* or during other nonsexual events.

But it's even worse for teenage girls.

Teenage girls start bleeding from places they've never bled from before. Happy-go-lucky daughters become angry, dramatic teens.

I should have known about these changes. But I didn't. I must have been daydreaming during sex-ed class. (For a long time, I also thought you peed out of your vagina.) Consequently, I freaked out the first time I got my period.

It's a good thing that I hit puberty before Google existed. I probably would have searched vaginal bleeding and convinced myself that I was dying. I've become a raging hypochondriac thanks to the power of Internet searching.

I was on vacation when I noticed some blood on the inside of my bathing suit. Blood was not a good sign. Most of my friends hadn't started their periods yet, so I was genuinely afraid for my life. I ran back to find my mom, who was sunbathing in a beach chair. She explained the joys of puberty and PMS.

I first truly experienced PMS a few months later, during an episode of *Buffy the Vampire Slayer*. Bad boy Spike had just confessed his love to Buffy. She turned and looked at love-struck Spike and callously spat, "I will NEVER love you."

That's when PMS first reared its ugly head in my life. I cried for two hours about the injustice of fate. "There is NOTHING sadder than unrequited love," I sobbed. My sister walked in and asked why I was crying like a fool.

I wailed, "YOU can't understand! It's the saddest thing in the—*sob*—whole—*whimper*—entire world."

And it felt like it too.

Until the next day.

The next day felt like the worst day of my life. I'm sure everything was running as per usual, but I could no longer deal with the norm. In my pubescent, hormonal mindset, everything in my life was going wrong. I had a crying fit in the bathroom during recess. I cried because I got a B on my math test. Because I wasn't cool. Because the week before I had lost my Trapper Keeper with my favorite Lisa Frank folder.

On the bus ride home, I sat alone. I closed my eyes and dreamed I was someone else. I envisioned a life where I wasn't chubby and had a lot of friends. A life where boys actually liked me and I still had my Trapper Keeper.

I was PMSing. Hardcore. My real life wasn't so bad. On a normal day, I would be sitting in the front yard in my inflatable chair, reading a book. On a non-PMS day, I didn't give a shit that I didn't really fit in. On any other day, I knew that they sold Lisa Frank folders at the grocery store for a dollar and forty-nine cents. Boys didn't like me but I didn't care; I had shit to do and no time for that nonsense.

This day was different. This day, hormones were running the show.

I came home and planned on drowning my PMS angst and sorrow in the usual fashion, by shoving my face full of food. My drug of choice: sugared cereal. After throwing my book bag on the floor, I ran to the kitchen and grabbed a box of Honey Nut Cheerios. I pulled out a bowl and began to pour in the cereal.

As I tipped the box toward my bowl, a cascade of crumbs flooded out of the package. I pulled the plastic bag out of the cardboard box.

Crumbs. The bag was full of crumbs. There wasn't a single Cheerio to be seen.

Then the rage came.

I looked at the unfilled cereal bowl, and then at the box. I saw red. Bright, angry red. All the stress of the day, the stress of being young, the stress of being me, came to a head and popped. My jaw clenched. I flexed my fists. Suddenly I turned into the Hulk and grabbed both sides of the cereal box. As if I were tearing the heaviest material on the planet, I furiously ripped the box in half while yelling, "Is it so hard to throw away the stinking box when you're done with it? Is it!? OH MY GOD!"

I grabbed the ripped pieces and tore them into more pieces while launching them angrily at the floor. "The trash can is right there, right freaking there! How stinking hard is it?" I screamed, enraged, spit flying from my mouth.

Then suddenly, this pathetic attempt at snacking was somehow a metaphor for my life. I couldn't get anything I wanted. Even something like cereal was unobtainable for someone like me. Suddenly, I was no longer angry. I was just very, very sad. I fell in the most dramatic way possible onto the floor. Assuming the fetal position, I began to cry hysterically. I cried for Spike. I cried for my Trapper Keeper. I cried about the dog shit on my pants a few months before. But mostly, I cried because I really wanted some cereal.

My older sister found me five minutes later in this position. With great concern she asked, "Oh my God. What's wrong? Want me to get Mom?"

In between sobs, I managed to get out, "I just—*sob*—wanted—*sob*—some Cheerios."

She stared at me for moment, assessing the situation. She looked down at me, contemplating what to say. She settled on, "You better get your ass up off that floor right now. If I ever see you crying that way ever again, you better be dying."

"Shut up! JUST SHUT UP! You don't know me!" I screamed back at her.

"Whatever." She said, walking away.

I continued crying on the floor for another ten minutes before my sobs turned into whimpers. I whimpered for another two minutes before ending my tantrum. I slowly got up from the floor. I picked up my torn box pieces and threw them into the trash. Sniffling loudly, I blew my nose a few times. In the absence of cereal, I grabbed a pint of ice cream and started spooning it directly from the carton into my mouth. I grabbed some chocolate syrup and made a chocolate sundae on my tongue. After ten minutes, my sugar rush kicked in and I felt better. The world was at peace again.

So yeah, being a teenage girl was a scary thing. It was scary because it involved a lot of blood in weird places. But it was also scary because it meant freaking out about cereal.

In PMS world, small problems become giant catastrophes. PMS emotions are unreal, exaggerated, and highly dramatic. I wish I could say it ends after puberty but it doesn't.

I'm in my mid-twenties and when I'm PMSing, I still go a little crazy. I get irrationally annoyed by things like unexpected ATM fees, slow drivers, and spotty Wi-Fi. On normal days, these things are mild irritations. On PMS days, they cause enraged meltdowns.

So, the best way to make being a woman a little less scary is to acknowledge it and deal accordingly.

And keep a fully stocked pantry of Cheerios.

Grocery Store Mama Drama

To understand who I am, you need to look at where I come from. My family is kind, tolerant, and supportive.

They're also highly neurotic and crazy. Even if I wanted to, I couldn't escape my neuroses. The dice were loaded from the start.

I was genetically destined to be weird.

I've already described my father's paranoia about doorbell ringers. My sister had her own fears as well. She was deathly afraid of vampires and made us tape crosses all over our beds with blue electrical tape. My stepdad is the most normal one of us all.

Which only leaves my mother.

My mom is a strong and compassionate woman. She's four feet eleven with the personality of a giant. She taught me how to be independent and kind. She taught me how to tell a good story and make people laugh. She's loved me unconditionally my entire life.

But if there's one thing you need to understand about my mother, it's that she's not a lesbian midget. Even though she's been called one.

My mom has been called a lesbian midget one time and one time only. I would be lying if I said it wasn't warranted.

It was warranted because of what happened with Louise. In the moment directly before anyone questioned my mother's sexuality, we were avoiding Louise like it was our full-time job.

The whole thing started at a grocery store in Ohio. We had been shopping there for eight years, for no reason other than it was the closest one to our house. There was nothing special about this grocery store. Bakery section. Produce section. Deli section. It wasn't trendy or organic. It didn't have a coffee bar or a beer station. It was part of a commercialized, conglomerate chain of grocery stores. We were ok with that.

Over these eight years, our family had developed a relationship with a cashier named Louise. She was a small, friendly black woman with gray hair and a giant smile. She had a loud voice and always shouted "Hey, GIRL!" from a foot away. If Louise's line was long, we waited the extra fifteen minutes just to get checked out by her. She was hilarious and always had a perfect one-liner ready to ease off her tongue. She stashed extra coupons under the register to ensure that we got the best deal on toilet paper.

There is something nice about familiarity; Louise always remembered our names and what was going on in our lives. She asked about school and our latest vacation. When my sister was going to prom, Louise asked, "Now, did Donny Stitzel buy you the blue corsage you wanted?" If my mom got a new haircut, she would say, "The new do looks so good, girl!"

I never asked her any questions back. I was too selfish and young to care about Louise's life. I was busy reading gossip magazines and grabbing a candy bar. But my mom would inquire about Louise and her sons. They would chat until all the groceries were sitting cozy in brown paper bags.

When I was fifteen, Louise's son was desperately seeking a job. My mom was the director of a company and, conveniently for Louise, was also doing the hiring. After eight years of developing a pretty decent grocery-line rapport, Louise pleaded with my mother to get her "wonderful and amazing" son an entry-level job.

"Jerome's such a hard worker; he would really be a great fit anywhere. He's so good with people," she gushed while scanning a can of soup.

"Sounds like a good fit," my mother said, handing Louise her business card. "Tell him to send me his résumé."

Jerome sent his résumé the following morning. He seemed like a prime candidate for an open entry-level job and my mom was happy to help Louise. She forwarded his C.V. to human resources.

Unfortunately, Jerome failed the background check. Despite being a nice kid, Louise's son had a driving record that made Lindsay Lohan look like Jesus. Driving was a big part of the job and there was no doubt that Louise's son would be a liability. For the safety of the clients, my mom was unable to hire him.

It's awkward anytime a friend asks you to do a favor involving their kids. In my mom's case it was even worse, because no one can tactfully say, "Your son is a hazard to every man, woman, child, plant, robot, and nonliving thing on the road. If anyone ever asked me, I would tell them to revoke his license permanently and not even let him near a bike."

No, you can't say that. So my mom did what any normal human being would do.

She avoided Louise like her life depended on it.

Suddenly, going to the grocery store became a workout. We were straining our necks and our ears looking out for Louise. When we heard her signature "HEY, GIRL!" yelled to some unknown face, we ducked down the condom aisle, *Frogger*-style. We made 180 degree turns back toward the deli, which we had already visited.

Avoiding someone is an exhausting task that incites quite a bit of paranoia. We were strategic, alert, and nimble. We learned how to turn a cart at a moment's notice and maneuver in-between two unknowing shoppers. We hid behind magazine racks and large cereal displays. We were skilled masters of the game "Operation Avoid Louise."

On what would ultimately turn out to be our last visit to this grocery store, we had cleared the produce section without any sign of her. I ducked my head down by the soups. Finding the coast clear, we beelined for some split pea and chicken noodle. An hour later, we had successfully filled our cart with two hundred dollars' worth of groceries without any run-ins. We carefully tiptoed around the bread and scurried toward the checkout. Thinking we were in the clear, we began unloading our cart.

We threw our caution to the wind. We started laughing and talking again, looking at trashy tabloid magazines while the cashier checked us out.

In the last stretch of the race, Louise entered stage left for the dramatic final scene. My mom, reaching into her wallet, heard an enthusiastic yet bone-chilling "Hey, Girl!"

Surprise shot up my mother's face. She slowly turned around, her wallet hanging from her hand. Less than a foot away, Louise was grinning brightly.

"Hey, Louise!" my mom said in that fake I'm-pretending-to-be-happy-to-see-you voice.

Louise took a step closer. She wasn't trying to be intimidating; on the contrary, she was always friendly and enthusiastic. She was just one of those people who had no concept of personal space. She always stood just a little bit too close.

"Did you have a chance to look at Jerome's résumé? He is so excited about the job!" she said, her spittle spraying my mom's nose.

My mother took a step backward and said, "I did look at it but unfortunately, we have very strict driving record regulations."

Louise took another step forward. She was a foot away from my mother's face. My mom backed up again. She was trapped against the gum display with nowhere to go. Confusion spread across Louise's face as she subconsciously took another step forward, only six inches away now.

"What do you mean, girl? Jerome's driving record is perfect."

My mom's face contorted. I watched helplessly as she struggled to find the right words.

Always a master of tact, she replied, "I'm so sorry, Louise, but his driving record came back with some issues that will prevent us from hiring him."

Louise took a final step forward. What happened next cannot be explained with any logical reasoning. When my mom told this story later, she tried to rationalize about what caused her to do what she did. Louise's face kept coming closer until she was only about a few inches away. My mother's face was ridden with anxiety.

Then my mom leaned forward. Confused, I leaned over to my sister and asked, "What the heck is mom doing?"

Before anyone could say anything else, she puckered and planted a big, fat kiss on Louise's cheek.

Louise's face lit up with shock. She stared at my mom, even more confused than before.

An awkward moment of silence passed.

Forgetting the current conversation about her son, Louise said, "Alright. Ok. Well, girl, it was good seeing ya. I...umm...I gotta run. Bye."

My mom's face turned bright tomato red.

My sister and I were still trying to figure out what had happened.

"Why did you just kiss Louise?" my sister asked.

"I don't know!" Mom was flustered.

"The only people that close to my face are my husband and my kids. It was a subconscious reaction," she continued, frazzled and embarrassed.

My sister and I, the Queens of Compassion, laughed until we were blue in the face.

She tried a million times to explain her actions. But it didn't matter what the explanation was; she had kissed Louise. So, logical excuse or not, we still had to switch grocery stores.

My mom claimed that our new grocery store had a "better selection," and that's why we were switching.

But we all knew the truth.

"It's because everyone thinks you're a lesbian midget, isn't it?" my sister asked one day.

"No. The other store doesn't have the milk I like to buy."

"Mom, milk is the same everywhere."

"Ok! Fine! It's because everyone thinks I'm a lesbian midget. Happy? I'm telling you, she was too close to my face. I didn't know what to do."

We laughed as she continued to rationalize.

Our new grocery store only hired acne-ridden sixteen-year-olds. Every time we checked out, we had a new cashier. We failed to develop grocery rapport with any of them. We were ok with that.

PART 2: ALL GROWN UP (OR SOMETHING LIKE THAT)

The awkward kid falls in love and then heads to college... but still can't manage to bone anyone.

Brazilian Broken Hearts

My first love was a Brazilian boy named Gustavo. He broke my heart four times. I let him do it because I was desperately, madly in love with him.

The craziest thing about falling in love is that it can happen on a day like any other day. It could happen at the grocery store or at the post office. It's never expected, but when it happens it changes your life forever.

In a lot of ways, the day I fell in love was a Saturday like any other Saturday. I woke up, brushed my hair, and ate my breakfast.

In a lot of ways, it was different too. Namely because I was living in São Paulo, Brazil, as a foreign exchange student.

When I graduated high school, I wanted to have a grand adventure before starting college. I decided to take a gap year and study abroad in Brazil.

I was eighteen and staying with a host family in the mountains outside of the world's third-largest city. I had spent the first six months of my exchange struggling to learn Portuguese and kissing copious amounts of Brazilian boys. For whatever reason, I woke up that Saturday in a high state of carpe diem. I decided that I needed to spend my final six months exploring São Paulo and visiting every Brazilian landmark I could.

I called my friend Marcus to see if he wanted to go to the São Paulo Zoo that afternoon. He reluctantly agreed. We were going to meet at his house and head to the zoo together. I threw on some tennis shoes, twisted my hair in a bun, and ran out the door.

If I had known I was going to fall in love, I might have dressed a little nicer.

Marcus was from Sweden and wasn't known for his punctuality. Like me, he was late everywhere he went, so, when I arrived (on time for once), he hadn't even showered yet.

"Sorry. I was expecting you to be late. I'll be quick. You can get on the computer while you're waiting if you want," Marcus said in his thick accent.

I sat down at his host family's computer, putzing around on the Internet to kill time. I was updating my travel blog when I heard footsteps approach the door. A deep male voice behind me said, "Hey, I'm Gustavo. I'm Marcus's host brother," in rich, smooth Portuguese. His voice melted over me as I spun around to meet my visitor. As my eyes hit his face, my jaw dropped.

I was looking at the most beautiful man I had ever seen. He was a golden specimen of the human race. His face was perfectly symmetrical and framed by high cheekbones. He had large, dark eyes that radiated Latino heat and sensuality. His full lips smiled to reveal perfectly white teeth against his dark-brown skin. He represented the kind of aesthetic beauty that Brazil is famous for.

"Holy. Fucking. Shit," I thought. I blinked a few times, trying to recover my thoughts. It was the first time I had ever been awestruck by anyone's beauty.

"Hi. I'm Olive," I managed to say.

"It's a pleasure to meet you." He grinned.

His attractiveness was overwhelming. Intimidating even. I couldn't form coherent thoughts or sentences. So I said the only thing that came to my mind.

"Wanna go to the zoo today?" I blurted out.

"Sure. Sounds fun. Let me grab a coat," he responded as he turned to leave the room.

"Dear God, that kid is stunning," I muttered to myself after he left.

Gustavo, Marcus, and I headed to the São Paulo Zoo together. As we bonded over the first monkey I had seen all trip, I was instantly drawn to him. Not only was he insanely attractive, he was funny and kind. When he spoke, his words were gentle and sincere in a way that made me trust and believe him.

Gustavo was curious and fascinated by foreign culture. He asked me a million questions about my life as an American. Like most Brazilian men, he was intrigued by a gringa. Under normal circumstances, I would have never had a chance with someone like Gustavo. But being foreign gave me an edge. Brazilian men love American women.

I turned up the charm to the highest level I could muster. I could tell he found me interesting and enjoyed my company. Every time I spoke Portuguese, he smiled, laughing at my accent. When we returned home from the zoo, Gustavo invited me to stay for dinner. I happily obliged.

I started making excuses to hang out at Marcus's more. Anytime Marcus and I made plans, I begged him to invite Gustavo. Gustavo usually came.

"You know he has a girlfriend, right?" Marcus asked me one day at lunch, shoving rice and beans into his mouth.

"Ya, I know. I don't *like* him or anything. He's just my friend," I said, trying to convince myself.

A few weeks later, I met Gustavo's girlfriend, Juliana. In the same way he was the most beautiful man I had ever seen, Juliana was the epitome of a Brazilian beauty with long, silky hair and dark-brown skin. She had a butt that made men drool. She had the kind of body that men masturbate to in magazines they hide from their wives. She was part Brazilian and part Japanese, with the best genetic traits from both sides. Together, they were perfectly perfect tens.

I hated her.

Except she was too nice to hate.

My friendship with Gustavo continued to deepen. After a few months, we were hanging out three or four times a week, often without Marcus. I frequently had dinner with his family and spent the night in their spare guest room.

One day while eating in the mall food court, his eyes intently focused on his food, he said, "I think you're the best friend I've ever had. I don't know what I'm gonna do when you go home."

I felt my face get hot and laughed nervously. "Ya, you're my best friend too. We'll stay in touch."

"I wish you didn't have to leave," he said with uncharacteristic shyness.

We were in dangerous territory and we both knew it. He was in a relationship and we both respected that. I had met his girlfriend many times. We had never crossed any lines and he wasn't the kind of person who would cheat.

"Juliana and I have started fighting a lot lately. I'm just..."

He trailed off.

Now it was my turn to stare intensely at my food.

"I'm just not sure we're a good match," he continued. "When you and I are together, we're having so much fun. When I'm with her, I feel stressed out."

My heart clenched. I didn't know what to say. He was scanning my face, looking for my response. Underneath his gaze, I was wrestling with my own emotions. I could no longer deny it. I was falling in love with this boy.

I was in a moral dilemma. He was in a relationship and I knew I had to be a good person and say the right thing. So even though I didn't want to, I said, "Hmm. You should probably talk to Juliana about everything and see how you both feel. The only way you can work things out is to talk."

He sat silently for a second, picking at his rice, before saying, "Ya. You're right."

I decided to avoid him for a few weeks. While I was busy trying to talk myself out of being in love, I assumed he was busy trying to salvage his three-year relationship.

One day, I logged on to MSN and he messaged me immediately.

"Hey! Haven't seen you in a while!"

"Ya, I've been super busy," I lied.

"I broke up with Juliana," he wrote.

I froze. I reread his message a dozen times to make sure I wasn't misreading it.

"Oh. I'm sorry to hear that," I typed.

"No, it was a good choice. I don't think we were a good match," he said back.

"Are you free next week? Wanna go to the movies?" he asked.

"Sure, sounds great."

On the day of the movies, I spent an extra hour getting ready, carefully applying my mascara and eyeliner.

I was nervous.

Despite seeing Gustavo frequently, I knew this time was different.

During the movie, the sexual tension was flowing between our bodies. I couldn't focus because I was trying to work up the courage to hold Gustavo's hand. I laid my hand openly on the armrest between us. He placed his hand next to mine, barely touching it, his pinky grazing my pinky. I felt a surge of heat through my body and wrapped my littlest finger around his.

At eighteen, falling in love is a fast journey. I didn't have any serious wounds or scars from past lovers. I wasn't jaded or apprehensive; I was completely baggage-free. So, I ran full force, with an open and vulnerable heart, into the teenage pool of love. I was bathing recklessly in infatuation.

By the end of the second month, he told me he loved me. Every day after that he would say, "Did I already tell you today that I love you?" I grinned the way that only people in love do.

I was living in a goddamned Nicholas Sparks movie.

I no longer walked places; I floated. I whistled everywhere I went, radiating happiness. I wanted to doodle his name on every notebook I had, but instead I etched it again and again in my mind, daydreaming about him every minute I was awake. Sometimes I didn't believe it was really happening to me. I was a former fat kid who no boy had ever liked.

For the first time in my life, I was the girl someone wanted.

And the boy who loved me was a perfect package. I felt like I had won the lottery.

We never consummated the relationship. We were both virgins and too afraid to do the deed. (If I had known that my vagina was going to stay penis-less for another six years, I probably would have jumped his bones after the movies.) But I was young, scared, and deathly afraid of what was going to happen after I left Brazil.

The week before I left, I was filled with emotion. I was excited to see my friends and family again at home. Mostly, I was sad about leaving Gustavo.

His family was taking me to the airport so I stayed with them the night before I left. Snuggling on his couch, I was too afraid to ask the question that needed to be asked.

"What…what's gonna happen to us?" I asked shyly into his collar.

"What do you mean?" he asked, kissing my cheek.

"You know, it's really far. What if you meet someone cooler than me?"

"That would never happen. Besides, I'm going to marry you."

I believed every word he said and smiled with the hope and delusion that only young, unbroken people can feel.

At the airport, I tried not to cry until I saw him crying. Airports are bittersweet for me. I'm always leaving people and places that I love to return to other people and places I love. We hugged for a long time, neither of us saying anything.

"See you in Ohio. I promise I'll visit soon," he whispered in my ear.

I nodded.

He kissed me and said, "Hey! Did I tell you yet today that I love you?"

I laughed. "You did not."

"Well I do!"

We said our final goodbyes and I turned to get on the plane.

After I settled into my flight, I started crying again. The lyrics "I'm leaving on a jet plane, don't know when I'll be back again" kept circling in my head.

After I returned home, Gustavo sent me an email every day that summer. I read each one fifty times, until they were ingrained in my memory. We talked on MSN for hours, hogging our family computers. We both believed we could make it work. We believed that we were different from every other couple who had tried long distance and failed. I thought he was my soul mate.

Two months later, I started my freshman year of college. While other girls in my dorm were getting wasted at frat parties, I was naked webcam-ing a boy thousands of miles away. My roommate caught me red-faced and embarrassed, shoving my boob back in my shirt.

"Talking to Gussssttaaavvvvooo?" she asked, throwing her purse on the bed.

She'd wave to him in the webcam and he'd wave back.

I spent the first semester of college glued to my computer. Although I had plenty of friends and an active social life, talking to Gustavo was my number one priority. I wrote him thoughtful letters and took pictures of my college campus and my friends.

This continued until late November, when I noticed a subtle change in communication. His daily emails started coming every three or four days. His beautiful love letters turned into formulaic blurbs. "Blah, blah. Miss you. Love you. Can't wait to see you." When I tried to talk to him about the changes, he told me I was being paranoid and it was just the distance. He reassured me that he still loved me. He promised that he would come visit. But I couldn't get rid of the nagging feeling that something was off. I tried to talk myself out of it but women's intuition is usually accurate.

Sure enough, I found out from a mutual friend that he was back with Juliana. I read the message and was too upset to go to class. I hopped in my car and frantically drove to a convenience store to buy a new long-distance phone card. I called him, unable to get the words out.

"Are you dating Juliana?" I struggled to ask. There was a long silence on the other end of the phone.

"I was terribly lonely without you."

It was the first time he broke my heart.

He cried too and promised he would end things with her again. Despite the pain and betrayal that I felt, more than anything, I still loved him. I was a hopeless, delusional romantic, brainwashed by a childhood full of too many Disney movies. I was angry and hurt but I still wanted to be with him. Losing him permanently was the worst thing that could happen. In my mind, the sun shined out of his ass. He was the filet mignon of all meats, the tiramisu of all desserts.

So I forgave him and we tried again.

It was never the same though. Long-distance relationships are really hard. Particularly for horny eighteen-year-olds. We could only cycle through old memories for so long. We started running out of things to say. By spring, it was clear to everyone but me that I was clinging to something that was no longer working. He had drifted away, and although we never "officially" broke up, we were hardly dating.

I couldn't give up. I was too wrapped up in the idea of him. Anytime I considered letting go, I reread his old love letters. "It will be fine once we're back together," I told myself.

I mean, I saw the fucking *Notebook*. True love always wins, damn it.

As the end of my freshman year rolled around, he was accepted into a six-month study-abroad program in Canada. He planned to visit me in Ohio for two weeks before heading to the Great White North. I was convinced that distance was our only problem, and the minute he saw me, he would immediately fall back in love.

I was living at home for the summer. My liberal hippie mom lectured me on the importance of safe sex. We went together to buy my first pack of birth control. I felt uncomfortable the entire time. Particularly when she handed over the small pink packet and said, "Better to be safe than pregnant! We can't have a little Olive running around."

When I saw him at the airport, my heart skipped a beat. I hadn't seen him in over a year. He was even better looking than I remembered.

He ran over and hugged me, casually kissing my cheek. While he was happy to see me, it wasn't the passionate reunion I had envisioned. That first evening, we stayed up all night talking. We laughed and reminisced as good friends do.

That was the problem. He was treating me like a friend. There were no lingering touches or loving glances.

The next day was the same. I decided to turn up the charm. He was friendly but still kept me an arm's length away. By the end of his first week in Ohio, I was desperately trying to make him remember how much he loved me. I didn't have the courage to tell him how I was feeling, so I instead I was overbearingly affectionate and kind. I wanted him to see how good of a person I was and remember how lucky he was to be with me.

That night, I sat in my bed and listened to him snoring in the guest bedroom. In my fantasies, he would softly knock on my door, and then crawl into my bed to cuddle. In reality, he was content to sleep alone.

I sneaked out of my room and stood in his doorway.

"Hey, are you up?" I asked despite the fact that he obviously wasn't.

He rolled over and sleepily mumbled.

"Can I join you?"

There was a long pause that made me doubt if he was awake.

"Sure," he said quietly.

I crawled into bed, careful not to touch him. We lay next to each other for several minutes, neither one moving. I could feel my heart palpitating in my chest. I leaned in quickly, before I lost my nerve, and started kissing him. He kissed me back with hesitation. His resistance stung me like a knife. It was too hard to be honest with myself that he didn't want to kiss me. So instead, I started kissing his shoulder and stomach, working my way down toward his pants.

"I'm not sure this is a good idea," he said.

I ignored him and toyed with the elastic on his boxers. I reached over and grabbed some scented lotion next to the bed.

"Are you sure you can use that?" he asked, eyeing the lotion skeptically.

"Ya, ummm, sure." I said.

"Olive, are you sure though? Like, seriously."

"Ya. Sure, of course. It will be fine." I said, smiling.

I squirted a large amount into my hand and onto his penis.

He immediately started yelling in Portuguese.

"Holy shit! Oh my God. It's burning me!"

"WHAT!?"

"FUCK. It's burning my dick," he cried in pain as I watched his erection immediately die.

"Oh shit!"

"Fuck, I'm gonna get in the shower," he said, his face scrunched in pain.

Thus far, that's the only time I've burned someone's penis.

I didn't know if I should stay in the room or go back to my bed, so I opted to stay there to make sure he was ok. He walked back into the room fifteen minutes later with a towel wrapped around his waist. He sat next to me on the bed.

Surprisingly, he was smiling.

"I knew you couldn't use that lotion," he said, laughing.

I started laughing too.

"It's lotion, who knew you couldn't use it?" I said.

"I knew!" he replied.

We laughed for a few more minutes, then I reached over and touched his hand.

He looked down, a mixture of guilt and sadness covering his face.

"Olive...I'm so sorry. I just...we can't do this. I will always love you...but we can't do this. The distance and the missing. It's too much."

I took my hand off his and looked away from his face.

"I'll move. When you get back from Canada. I'll move to Brazil," I said.

"You can't do that. You're in the middle of college."

I knew he was right. I knew that quitting school wasn't an option. I couldn't face reality.

I sat silently for a moment, trying to digest what was happening.

"What about the beautiful things you said to me? Did you mean any of it?" I asked accusingly.

I was being dramatic. If Taylor Swift can write a hit song about each of her past lovers, I deserved to be dramatic once in a while too.

"Of course I meant it. I did love you. I meant all of it...but..." he trailed off.

It was the second time he broke my heart.

Past tense. He had loved me. I heard him but I didn't comprehend it. How could you love someone and then not? Poof, done. Simple as that. I couldn't accept it.

Unintentionally Celibate

He left for Canada the next week.

"You're my best friend," he said at the airport as he waved goodbye.

Just like that, my first love friend-zoned the shit out of me.

A few nights later, I was sitting around with some friends, drinking and playing Apples to Apples, when someone said, "Man, I miss Gustavo. That guy was great." Everyone else chimed in with a glowing review of their own.

"You like him more than me!" I screamed, slamming my cards onto the table. "Nobody even cares that he broke my heart," I yelled while running out the door in order to cry hysterically. I was an emotional wreck for weeks after that.

I wish I could make myself seem less pathetic and say that I was in my right mind. I wish I could say I was totally over him. But I wasn't.

By the start of my sophomore year, I was interested in physical pursuits only. In terms of love, I was emotionally exhausted. Although I wasn't naked webcam-ing Gustavo, I still thought about him often. I focused on my schoolwork and my social life. On cold evenings, I kept myself occupied by making out with a douchey redhead. On lonely days, Gustavo always crept back in my mind.

We talked occasionally on instant messenger but not with any sort of regularity. I tried to drown the thoughts of him. I forced myself not to reread his old letters anymore.

After six months in Canada, Gustavo returned to Brazil. I knew it wasn't healthy but I still checked his MSN messenger status occasionally for updates.

That was how I found out that he had fallen in love with a Canadian.

It was the third time he broke my heart. It wasn't his fault but I couldn't help how angry and hurt I felt. It was the ultimate betrayal.

If I wasn't so angry about it, I might have found the irony comical. For months, he had told me how long distance was too painful and then he went and fell in love with a Canadian. I snooped around and found out that her name was Bobby Sue. I scowled in disgust. Goddamned Canadians with their two first names. In the good ol' United States of 'Merica, only people in West Virginia without teeth have two first names.

I prayed that Bobby Sue was missing a tooth.

She wasn't.

She was a gymnast with a perfect body and all of her teeth. I studied her picture for an hour, comparing myself to her and generating the most self-pity I could muster. I couldn't help but be jealous. She became my nemesis. She had everything I wanted but couldn't get: a perfect body; long, enviable legs; and, most important, my Brazilian. She won; I lost.

I spent that entire night crying in the parking lot outside my dorm.

It was a scenario I would repeat a lot the following year.

Despite my anger over Bobby Sue, it wasn't enough to help me forget Gustavo. There's a magic sort of power connected to a first love. So even though I casually dated throughout the rest of college, I couldn't fully get over him. No one even compared. It was like eating at a five-star restaurant, and then being forced to eat at McDonald's. Every man after Gustavo left a bad aftertaste.

I knew it was crazy but, despite everything, I still thought that maybe, just maybe, we would end up together. The practical voice in my head couldn't quite kill the hope of the eighteen-year-old who had had adventures and felt loved. So when I graduated college, I decided that as a graduation gift to myself I was going back to Brazil for Carnival.

Gustavo was excited that I was coming back to visit and told me I could stay with him and his family. He was still dating The Canadian. They had managed to maintain a long-distance relationship for over two and a half years. I couldn't help but feel bitter that she was worth doing long distance with and I wasn't.

When my friends asked me if I thought anything was going to happen upon my return, I always responded with, "Nah, we're just good friends." But the undying and delusional "just maybe" was still in the back of my mind. I could have fueled Barack Obama's entire campaign with my hope.

Six months before graduation, I hired a personal trainer. I didn't have two first names but I'd be damned if I didn't get a chiseled body. If I was going back to Brazil, I was going to look the best I possibly could. I think I believed that maybe if I had a body like Bobby Sue, he would love me again. I thought that maybe if his friends thought I was hot, so would he. We just needed more time together and he would remember.

I paid a pretty penny for my trainer and it showed. By the time I went to Brazil, I was looking good. Despite the thirteen-hour plane ride, I exited the plane looking fresh. I walked confidently toward the baggage claim where I saw him standing.

"Olive?" he asked.

"Hey!" I exclaimed, heading in for a hug.

"I didn't recognize you. You look really great!" he said.

I smiled. Everything was working according to plan.

Over the course of the next few weeks, it became clear that he loved me.

In the friend sort of way.

Bobby Sue's picture was sitting in a frame next to his bed, where my picture once sat. She won again. I wondered where he had shoved my picture.

Three days later, when he mentioned proposing to my archrival nemesis, Bobby Sue, the "just maybe" died on the spot; little traces of my eighteen-year-old heart were found at the scene of the crime.

It was the fourth time he broke my heart.

This time, I was the only person to blame. I congratulated him and really tried to mean it.

The next night at a party, I rebounded by making out with his friend Fernando. While cuddling with someone I didn't care about or even like, I came to the sad realization that I didn't really belong in Gustavo's life anymore. And vice versa. It was truly time to move on.

I left Brazil a little more cynical than I had been the first time. I was glad to return home to boring old Ohio, where people shook hands instead of kissing to greet each other. I was annoyed with and tired of Brazilian men. When I was young, I found their prose and flattery charming. This time around, I found it disingenuous. When I was eighteen, the Brazilian practice of kissing several strangers a night seemed exciting. At twenty-two, I was paranoid about oral herpes. In my teens, I thought long distance was romantic. At twenty-two, I thought, "Wouldn't it be nice to have someone to go grocery shopping with." When I returned home, I buried the pieces of my eighteen-year-old heart and allowed myself to regenerate a new one that was a little less naïve but still open. For the first time in years, my mind was free of lingering thoughts about my first love.

For the next several years, Gustavo and I communicated sporadically. He would wish me a happy birthday and I would send his family a Christmas card. He called occasionally and we would catch up as if no time had passed at all, but we didn't go out of our way to make the effort.

When I turned twenty-five, he was visiting New York, where I was living and dating a musician. He contacted me to meet up with him for drinks. At one point in my life, I would have dropped everything, blown off my friends, quit my job, and entirely rearranged my schedule to see him. This time, I was refreshingly indifferent. It would be nice to see him but I wasn't going to inconvenience myself.

We met at a bar on the Upper West Side, around the corner from my house. He brought a beautiful Brazilian girl with him and introduced her as his girlfriend. I was mildly surprised by this turn of events but shrugged it off, since it really wasn't my business.

We ordered a pitcher of beer and laughed like old friends do, reminiscing about funny memories.

"Remember the lotion?" he said in English so his girlfriend, Ana, couldn't understand, his face breaking into a wide grin.

"How could I forget," I said, laughing. "Sorry about that."

I was surprised by how much fun it was seeing him again. It reminded me of why I had once loved him in the first place. I felt no longing or sadness but only the kind of happiness that comes from reconnecting with someone you've known a long time.

When his Brazilian girlfriend went to the bathroom, I couldn't contain my curiosity. "What happened with Bobby Sue?" I asked in Portuguese.

"Oh. Um. It's a long story," he said, laughing, with a hint of sadness in his eyes.

"Sum it up before Ana comes back."

"She's dating a girl."

I was speechless. Of all the possible scenarios that had gone through my head, that one had never been a remote possibility. For years, I had hated this girl simply because he had loved her more than he'd loved me. For years, she had been my nemesis, with her perfect gymnast body and her two first names.

"What do you mean?" I asked, still not comprehending clearly.

"Her girlfriend's name is Jenny. She's a lesbian," he reiterated.

His current girlfriend walked back to the table and we quickly changed the subject, though my mind was still trying to process this new information.

We parted ways and said our goodbyes, knowing that we would see each other again in a few years.

Later that night, I was lying in bed thinking about all of it. It was crazy that somehow it had all worked out— though not in the way any of us had imagined. We were all dating new people and happy with our current situations.

Maybe life isn't a Nicholas Sparks movie after all. It's a comedy.

I'd choose a romcom over a drama any day.

The Party Pariah

(The Password Was Turtles)

I wanted to go to a raging frat party. Which meant I needed to find Chip.

Chip was a college legend, a god among men. During the first month of Chip's freshman year, he threw a "Pimps and Hoes" party that elevated him to celebrity status. The party had free-flowing liquor and scantily clad women. The best DJ on campus provided the music. That party made Chip the authority of all parties. From that night forward, anytime there was a crazy party on the frat-scene circuit, Chip was somehow involved.

I wasn't usually a frat-party kind of gal. Fraternities weren't my cup of tea: too many roofies and douche in one house. But there was a particular evening, at the age of twenty, when I wanted to find Chip and experience one of his raging parties.

College is a beautiful, wonderful place devoid of bills and responsibility. It's a lustrous haven where people can get up at one p.m. and go out for Thirsty Thursdays. It's a place full of educated people who enjoy drinking themselves into oblivion while hooking up with random strangers.

I started the night on the couch at Kate and Holly's college apartment. During a commercial break in a *Rock of Love Bus* marathon, I turned to Holly and said, "Dude, let's go to a frat party tonight."

Kate and Holly looked at me, surprised. We had been friends for years and I'd never been a big partier. Although they occasionally visited the scene, it was the first time I had expressed interest in joining them. For some reason, watching Bret Michaels for two hours triggered something foreign inside of me. I wanted to drink free beer provided by frat-boy assholes. I wanted to make out with someone who smelled like Abercrombie & Fitch. I wanted someone

69

handsome and tan to tell me I was hot while I drunkenly groped him.

"Ya sure. Let's call Rob," Holly said.

Rob was our only bro-style friend. He was our best link to the frat scene.

He came over twenty minutes later with his collar popped, a case of Natty Light, and the cell phone number for Chip.

"If we're gonna party hard tonight, we gotta call C-dawg. He'll be at the best one."

We opened some Natty and started pregaming while Rob dialed the number in his phone.

No answer.

Rob tried again.

Nothing.

He called Chip every five minutes for the next hour.

"Shit, guys. I have no idea where he could be. He's not answering his phone. Wanna just head over to his house?"

With no backup plan, we decided that was a great idea. Kate, Rob, and I piled into the car with our reluctant designated driver, Holly. With our buzz already on, we headed over to pay Chip an unexpected visit.

We drove for ten minutes and parked in front of a college rental house. Girls in short skirts and high heels littered the streets.

We were young and wanted to party, so we weren't thinking rationally. At the time, it didn't seem odd that we had to jump the fence to get into Chip's place.

Or that Chip's lights were off.

Or that Chip obviously wasn't there.

So we jumped the fence, waltzed in through the unlocked back door, and made ourselves comfortable on Chip's couch.

Rob turned on all the lights and the TV.

"Make yourselves at home. Chip's mad cool. He's probably upstairs taking a post-party, pre-party nap," he said, heading toward the fridge.

He grabbed a can of Bud Light and sprinted upstairs to search the bedroom for a presumably napping Chip.

Kate and I turned the channel to the *Rock of Love Bus* marathon and also helped ourselves to Chip's beer. We were reclining on the hand-me-down couch when Rob frantically ran downstairs yelling, "SHIT. We gotta go!"

"What the fuck are you talking about?" Holly asked.

"FUCK! It's the wrong apartment. GET OUT. WE'VE GOT TO GET OUT!" he shouted.

I looked toward Kate, who shrugged her shoulders and got up to leave. I scrambled off the couch and grabbed my purse. Holly scurried around, turning off the lights and making everything look untouched. Rob disappeared as Holly, Kate, and I ran out the door. Running as fast as she could toward the fence, Holly yelled, "Where's Rob?"

We all turned around and saw him emerging from the house with a six-pack he stole from the stranger's stash. We didn't stop running till we reached the fence and jumped over it as stealthily as we could. For no reason except the adrenaline high, we continued running for another two blocks before slowing down.

As we came to a stop, Rob pulled out a beer and started laughing.

"What the fuck was that about?" Holly asked, annoyed.

"Sorry, guys. I made a mistake, but at least I got us some free beer," he said while laughing and dialing Chip with his other hand. That was the kind of frat-boy mentality that I both admired and despised.

Rob took a swig of beer as he listened to Chip's voice mail for the sixteenth time.

"It's Rob. Call me back, asshole."

Uncertain of our next move, we saw a couple stumble toward us. We watched them enviously. They were obviously partaking in the kind of night we wished we were having.

"You guys lookin' for a party?" the drunk chick slurred. "That house over there is having one. Tell them you know Turtles."

"Thanks!" Rob said, high-fiving the girl.

"Alright, we got this. You're girls and you're hot. We can get in," Rob assured.

We started walking in the direction she'd pointed, toward a frat house. Beer cans littered the lawn and Greek letters were prominently displayed over the front door. There were two beefy bouncer guys with crossed arms blocking the entrance. I tried to suppress an eye roll. They were both wearing popped-collar shirts and obviously worked out and tanned a lot. This was before *Jersey Shore* but these guys were the "Situations" of the evening. They gave us a scrutinizing glance, and after thirty seconds of silence, one said, "Who do you know?"

Rob hesitated for a minute, and then with false bravado calmly stated, "Turtles."

We all held our breath as they whispered and finally decided that we were allowed to enter the party.

We walked excitedly into the house to discover six guys playing beer pong and no one else in sight. Two bouncers for six douches.

"Free beer in the fridge. The party was crazzzy, like, an hour ago," said one of the six.

We looked around and grabbed some free beer. It was possibly the lamest party I've ever been to. Upon the entrance of fresh female meat, one of the six guys tried to revive the party by suggesting everyone move to the basement. We were ushered downstairs to a dark room filled with disco lights and loud music. The ten of us started dancing and gyrating. A sweaty, blond guy came up behind me and started grinding on my back. I looked over and saw Kate making out with someone. It looked slobbery and unpleasant. I watched as he thrust his tongue unskillfully all over her face.

Blondie leaned over and whispered in my ear, "I want some titties in my mouth."

My suppressed eye roll surfaced. I laughed out loud while Holly, still sober, looked incensed about the whole situation.

"We can do better. Let's go," Holly texted me, even though she was only standing a foot away.

"Yep. Let's rally the troops," I texted back, sliding away from Blondie as he was getting ready to cop a feel.

"We're leaving," we yelled toward Rob and Kate, saving her from the slobberfest.

Rob was more than happy to leave, given the uneven male-to-female ratio.

We blitzed by the bouncers and headed for the sidewalk.

Once again, we were partyless.

"Don't worry, guys. The whole night will be awesome once we find Chip," Rob said.

"And how do you suggest we do that?" Holly asked with a biting tone.

"Ok. I'm thinking we should just drive around and look for signs of an awesome party. Like loud music, people outside. Lots of cars. Someone's bound to know where Chip is."

"That's literally the dumbest idea I've ever heard. Gas is expensive!" Holly said, turning to us for backup.

Unfortunately for Holly, Kate and I were less-than-sober and still wanted to party.

"I dunno. Sounds like a decent idea to me," I said.

"We'll chip in for gas," Kate assured, pulling a five out of her purse.

We drove in circles, on and off our college campus. After ten minutes, we passed a house that was booming with activity. Several partygoers stood outside on the porch, holding red cups and yelling loudly.

"Stop here," Rob demanded.

Holly scowled but turned around to look for a parking spot. We parked a block away and continued our mission to find the elusive Chip.

We had spilled out of the car and were stumbling toward the new party when we were accosted by a man with a bloody hand walking in the opposite direction. He was wearing a plaid kilt and a lot of eyeliner. His long hair was tied in a ponytail.

"Hey. Umm…someone just ran over my hand. Can I have a quarter?" he said in a feminine voice.

He was eerily calm for the way his hand was bleeding. He had a long scrape running down the length of it.

Kate wasn't nearly as calm. "Oh my God! Is your hand ok? You should really put some Band-Aids on that!"

What he really needed to do was go to the hospital. But in Kate's drunken state, Band-Aids seemed like they would solve the problem.

"It's fine. I really just need a quarter," he replied in a slow, drugged-out drawl.

"You need to take care of your hand! What happened?" asked Kate in a drunken panic. Ever the motherly type, she pulled out some tissues from her purse and handed them over.

"I was sitting on the curb over there and some guy just ran it over. I asked him for money but he gave me this bag of weed instead to make up for it," he said matter-of-factly, as if that explained anything.

"So...do you have a quarter or not?"

I was too shocked to respond.

"What the fuck...?" Rob muttered under his breath.

Thankfully, Kate managed to pull a quarter out of her purse and gingerly handed it over to the bleeding man.

"I have some dollar bills if you need them," Kate stated.

"Thanks, hon, but the quarter should be just fine," he said, strolling away slowly.

On the way to the party, we reflected on the situation and attempted to make sense of it. We tried and failed to decipher what he could have possibly done with one quarter.

We arrived at the party and walked inside like we knew everyone there. In our haste, we failed to assess the party guests. Everyone was dressed in black goth gear or vampire fetish attire. Most of the guys had long hair and a lot of makeup. It was glaringly obvious that we didn't belong.

We had just wandered into the kitchen and grabbed some PBRs when a heavily tattooed man asked, "Who the fuck are you?"

"Oh, we're friends with John," Rob lied with ease.

"There's no one fucking here named John. So you better fucking put my beer down."

"Chill out, man. We're just looking for a good time."

"By drinking MY beer."

"Sorry, dude. We didn't know."

"You think you can just crash any party you want and steal shit that's not yours?" he said, grabbing the beer out of Rob's hand and shoving him toward the fridge.

Holly and I exchanged glances quickly and decided it was time to hightail our asses out the door.

"Chill the fuck out, man," Rob said, shoving him back.

"We're so sorry. We're leaving now," Holly intervened, flashing her flawless apologetic smile.

We grabbed Rob's arm and raced toward the door, down the steps, and back toward our parked car, frantically checking to see if anyone was following us.

We arrived at the car alone. We were tired, relatively sober, and damn sick of trying to find a party. It was supposed to be an amazing evening but we were failing miserably. Designated driver Holly was getting irritable.

"This is stupid. We made a noble effort. Can we just go home and call it a night?" she pleaded.

"Just one more stop. I promise. Let's at least try to salvage the night. We'll go see some of Chip's main bros. If anyone will know where Chip is, they will. I promise, guys, they will know. It's all gonna be worth it," Rob reassured.

We rode in the car in silence, with Rob directing Holly where to go. We pulled in front of an old-looking house. It looked like it had suffered too many years of college students living carelessly. The paint was peeling and there were cigarette butts strewn all over the front stoop. A Cleveland Browns flag hung haphazardly from the window.

We walked up the steps and were once again disappointed. It was another filthy all-guy house that reeked of weed and stale beer. We walked in to find two guys lighting a bong and one passed out on the couch.

Looking toward the couch, Rob gestured angrily at the unconscious body and said, "What the hell happened?"

"Dude, calm down, brosef. Chip started drinking at eleven a.m. We came home after dinner and he was conked out on our couch. We think he climbed in through the fucking window, because the door was locked."

The weight of his words washed over me numbingly. I frowned and hung my head in defeat. "Goddamnit." I scowled.

Kate, the only one of us who was still drunk, asked, "Wait, what? Where's Chip and where's the party?"

Holly snapped back, "Don't you get it? That loser is Chip and there is no fucking party. We've been on a wild-goose chase all night!"

"Oh," said Kate as she hung her head too.

And just like that, the pariah Chip was just another wasted douche with no party.

"I'm hungry. Let's just go to Taco Bell," Kate suggested.

We all piled back into the car and headed toward the nearest TB. The evening ended anticlimactically with some Nachos Supreme. No making out. No half-naked people. Just some fake cheese. No *Animal House* stories of party wildness. No men smelling like Old Spice. Just raging disappointment and an empty gas tank.

My one goal for the evening, to go to an epic party, remained unfulfilled. I blamed Chip.

Maybe I'm a Lesbian

I never wanted to lick a vagina.

Until I met Julie French.

Prior to Julie French, I was pretty closed-minded about my own sexuality. One of my roommates sophomore year of college told me she was bisexual. I remember being mildly concerned that she would hit on me. I was nervous to be naked in front of her, afraid she would be checking me out. Before Julie French, I didn't understand how gray sexuality could be. In my mind, it was black-and-white.

I met Julie French during my junior year of college. She was the hottest lesbian I had ever known. She was tall and thin with a Justin Bieber haircut.

She was magnetic. Everyone either wanted her or wanted to be her, usually the former. Men and women alike. She was so cool that just being around her made you feel cool. She was smart, funny, and the center of attention. She had that devil-may-care attitude. She would glide up behind you, place a hand on your shoulder, and boldly whisper in your ear, "God, you look so sexy today." She chain-smoked hand-rolled cigarettes and wore sweatpants when everyone else was trying really hard to look cool.

We were both political science majors, which meant that we hung out with a lot of open-minded people. We liked to talk about world events and debate political happenings. We prided ourselves on being accepting and tolerant liberals.

Julie loved straight women. She was a self-proclaimed "turner." She loved the thrill of convincing a straight girl to give her a chance. She was the best turner on our university campus and had a list of seven straight girlfriends who dated men before and after her. Julie French (and we always called her by her full name) was the only person who ever made me truly and sincerely doubt my sexuality.

One night at a party, after drinking a lot of PBR, Julie sidled up beside me.

"You're looking pretty hot," she said, her lips touching my cheek.

"Thanks," I said, blushing.

"I want to kiss you," she said in a sexy drawl.

I didn't know what to do.

I wanted her to kiss me. My body was aroused by her touch.

I was afraid of the implications of this.

In my world, kissing Julie French and enjoying it meant I was a lesbian.

I started overanalyzing the situation, my mind racing with questions.

"What if I am a lesbian? Will I have to come out to my friends and family? Will they still accept me? Will they pretend to be cool with it but secretly afraid to get undressed in front of me? Will they think I'm attracted to them? Will I be forever marginalized by society? Will people start introducing me by saying, 'This is my friend Olive, she's a lesbian…'?"

While I was questioning my future, Julie was stroking my arm.

I laughed nervously and hopped out of my seat.

I wasn't ready to take the leap.

"Not tonight," I said.

"When?" she asked.

"Soon," I said flirtatiously, deferring any decision making for another day.

Later that night, I sat in my dorm bunk, pondering the thought of scissoring. I called my best friend in a total panic. I knew she would accept and love me no matter what, so I felt comfortable talking to her about it.

"Hey yo, what's shaking?" she said.

"Dude. I think I'm attracted to a girl."

Silence.

"Wait. Are you telling me that you're a lesbian, because that's totally cool if you are," she responded.

"Not exactly," I explained. "Just this one specific girl."

We talked about it for a while as she helped me sort out some of the confusion. We both decided I needed to call someone with more experience in this realm.

I called my good friend Patty, a bona fide lesbian.

"Hey, I have a kind-of weird question. When did you know you were attracted to women?"

Patty laughed.

"Why are you asking?"

"I think I might be a lesbian."

"I've been attracted to girls for as long as I can remember," Patty said, answering my question. "My earliest crush was in the third grade, on Mary Watson."

My earliest crush was on Trevor Smith. Every crush I'd ever had since then was a man, up until Julie French. The only person I'd ever been in love with, Gustavo, was decidedly male.

I filled her in on Julie.

"Hmmm. Sounds like it might just be this girl, huh?"

"I'm not sure; how do I know?" I asked sincerely.

"You just know, hon. Would you rather lick a penis or a vagina?"

"A penis," I said without hesitation.

"Then you're probably straight. Just because you have a crush on this one girl doesn't make you a lesbian. Sexuality is a spectrum."

I considered her statement. It made sense.

"What should I do about Julie?" I asked.

"Go for it. We're in college. Now's the time to experiment."

A week later, my friend James was throwing a party.

I put on a cool outfit and some high heels. I shaved my legs carefully and applied some lip gloss.

Tonight was the night.

I was going to kiss Julie French.

When I arrived, I hugged James and headed for the fridge. I needed some liquid courage.

I downed my first beer.

"That was fast," James noted.

"Where's Julie?" I asked.

"She was talking to Lauren in the living room," he said.

I pulled out some ChapStick and applied it.

I smacked my lips and headed out of the kitchen to find Julie.

I spotted her in the corner, kissing Lauren.

James walked over and followed my gaze.

"Didn't see that one coming," he said. "Though apparently, Julie's been hitting on Lauren for months. She broke up with her boyfriend a few weeks ago."

I nodded and headed outside. I was both relieved and sad.

I had missed my opportunity to explore my sexuality with the only woman I had ever been attracted to. I was never going to have the chance to say, "This one time in college..."

A few weeks later, I found out that Julie and Lauren had used fish sticks to pleasure each other that night. I'm still not exactly sure about the logistics of that (like, aren't fish sticks crumbly?) but it wasn't my business.

Julie and Lauren started dating and ended up in a long-term relationship for over three years.

After that, I was more open to the idea of sexuality. It's not as black-and-white as I had always thought. Honestly, I'm not opposed to the idea of exploring the female body.

Despite this, Julie was my first and last girl crush to date and I've never actually licked a vagina.

How Do You Accidentally Pick Up a Stalker?

I accidentally picked up a stalker once.

It was hailing that night and below zero. It was the coldest day of an already freezing winter.

Despite the weather, I was driving over to my friend's house for a relaxing game night.

I pulled out of my apartment complex and drove a few blocks, when I saw a woman wearing a Statue of Liberty costume.

Normal people might have questioned this situation. I'm not normal, so in my mind, this didn't seem odd at all.

She was *obviously* going to a patriotic theme party. I too was an avid theme-party-goer. I applauded her creativity. As I watched the hail mercilessly beat down on her, I mourned her ruined party costume.

Chilled to the bone from walking the short distance to my car, I sympathized that she must be freezing.

I'm a paranoid person and paranoid people never do things like let strangers into their cars. On that night, I wasn't thinking rationally. I went to college at Kent State University, a notoriously supportive community. I was living in false bubble of security. After all, someone dressed up like Lady Liberty seems perfectly harmless. And after all, she was probably only going a few blocks down. Offering her a ride was the kind thing to do.

I pulled over to the side of the road where she was walking and rolled down my window.

"Hey, you need a ride?"

She turned around rapidly and said, "Yes," in a chilling, deep, male voice.

In those few seconds, I realized that "she" was really a male in his late twenties.

Too shocked to reply, I watched helplessly as he entered my car and sat in the front seat. It became clear that he wasn't wearing a Statue of Liberty costume at all; instead it seemed like a long, silver cape. I examined him carefully, and suddenly everything seemed threatening. The rain dripping off his nose was terrifying. His unibrow screamed "unaware of social norms."

We sat silently for several seconds before I asked anxiously, "Where are you heading?" He smiled and it seemed menacing. I'm sure it was actually a perfectly normal smile, but in my mind he looked exactly like the Joker. He responded with the name of a town nowhere near the KSU campus, in an expressionless voice reserved for pedophiles and rapists.

Awesome. Not only did I have a crazy man in my car, he had the quintessential I'm-going-to-hurt-you-and-enjoy-it voice.

I began driving toward his destination in the neighboring town in silence before asking, "So, what's with the silver ensemble?"

"It's my space coat," he said as if that explained everything.

Just fucking great, a psycho in a space coat.

"I'm Darryl. What's your name?" he asked after I didn't respond.

As a gut reaction, I blurted out the first thing that came to my mind. When he asked me my name, at that moment it was Rachel. I was from South Dakota and I was studying architecture.

I rarely lie but I was concerned for my safety.

"Oh, that's cool. What do you love about designing buildings?" he asked.

"Ummmm. I love figuring out the details. You know, like, where you put a bathroom to make sure it's accessible yet out of the way." The lies fumbled awkwardly off my tongue.

"Where are you coming from at this time of night?" I asked, trying to change the subject from my obvious lack of architectural knowledge.

"I was at a Young Democrats meeting. I'm actually a Republican but the woman I love goes to those meetings," he explained. Right when I thought it couldn't get any worse, he was a Republican too.

"That's nice that you go there to support her. How long have you been together?" I said.

"Well...we're technically not together."

"Of course you're not," I thought. That would have been too normal.

"I love her but she's eighteen and it isn't really working out. Her parents don't approve."

If I wasn't already feeling uneasy, his honesty about his eighteen-year-old lover was unsettling. I tried to feign interest while secretly dialing my friend Tony so he could call the cops if necessary. I discreetly placed the phone in my lap, silently willing Tony to stay on the line.

"Eighteen isn't that young. How old are you?" I asked politely.

"Twenty-nine."

He turned and looked at me. "Do you think age matters, Rachel? Do you think it matters when you're in love?"

I considered my answer carefully. "Eleven years isn't that bad."

I didn't mean it, not in the slightest. I was actually thinking, "Yes, it matters when you're twenty-nine years old. What could you possibly have in common with a freshman in college?"

But I didn't say that because I didn't want it to be MY body found floating in the river two days later. He seemed like the kind of person who disposed of bodies in rivers.

Despite the cold air outside, I was sweating. My palms were clammy as I death-gripped the steering wheel. I calculated how far I was from his destination and watched the clock anxiously. Every instinct I had told me I was in danger. I silently prayed and promised I would never do anything this stupid ever again if I could just get out of this situation. I concentrated all my energy to send telepathic messages to Tony, who was listening silently on the line.

"It's a bummer that her parents don't approve. You seem like a nice guy," I lied.

"That's not really the problem. She doesn't love me," he said. He paused, more dramatically than necessary before saying, "I would treat her so well but she only loves assholes and bad boys."

He looked sad, and in that moment, I could tell there was a real human being inside the space coat. For one fleeting second, I felt genuinely bad for him.

"Have you ever been in love, Rachel?" he asked.

"Nope. Wouldn't know love if it punched me in the face," I joked. This was also a lie. It was one I didn't really need to tell, but I figured the less he knew about me the better off I was.

Then he asked a bone-chilling question: "Do you have Facebook? We should be friends."

"Oh God," I thought. "Shit. Fuck."

"Uhhhhhhhh…errr…noooope," I said. "I'm a private person."

Enough was enough. I wanted him out of my car, and fast. My heart was clenching with that take-action-or-die feeling. I did the only logical thing to do. I apologized profusely but explained that I was going to have to drop him off at a gas station. He seemed confused and a little hurt but I needed him out of my car.

"Sorry," I muttered, "I'm just super late," I said. I pulled away as he was barely out of the door.

The minute the door shut, I heard Tony yell from the cell phone in my lap, "Tell me you didn't fucking pick up a stranger. Tell me that's not what I just heard."

"I thought it was a girl in a Statue of Liberty costume," I said as if that explained the situation.

"Don't ever do that again. And if you do, don't call me. I don't want that responsibility. What the fuck was I supposed to do?" Tony screamed into the phone.

I apologized profusely and promised that I had learned my lesson.

When I arrived at game night, Tony had already told everyone his side of the story. I attempted to retell it from my perspective.

The general consensus was that I was a huge moron.

"When was the last time you went to a patriotic theme party?" Jeremy asked.

"Why was that your first thought? That's insane," Jay added.

Three months after the original incident, I joined some of my political science friends in the library for a thesis-writing party. I was sleep deprived and living on caffeine, so I barely registered the comment "She had to get a restraining order." I plopped down with a bag of Doritos and my computer.

"What are you guys talking about?" I asked through a yawn, leafing through some research material.

"We're all part of this club called the Young Democrats. There's this newbie freshman who just joined. Long story short, there's this creepy old guy who has been stalking her. Like, sitting outside her house and shit. I guess they dated for two weeks and he became totally obsessed. He's, like, thirty or something. And still in college.

She had to change her phone number and get a restraining order," my friend Danielle said.

My jaw dropped. "Fuck, is his name Darryl?"

"Yea! How did you know?" Danielle asked with large eyes.

"I gave that kid a ride in my car," I said. "He was wearing a space coat."

"Are you serious?" Danielle gawked.

"He was walking on the side of the road...and...it was perfectly logical at that point in time."

I relayed the entire story one more time. Once again, despite my best efforts at defense, everyone agreed that I was a moron.

I hoped the story would be laid to rest in the Graveyard of Totally Idiotic Ideas. Alas, most bad ideas and the stories that follow them have a way of remaining alive and intact for years to come. This was no exception. Much to my chagrin, it was retold at a party several years later for new sets of ears to hear. The story became sort of a legend. Even I started retelling it.

"There's hardly anything threatening about a patriotic woman going to a frat party. If you had been there, you would have done the same," I said.

But most people argued that they probably wouldn't have.

I hate to admit it, but that's probably true.

Gingerdouchesupreme vs. Edward Cullen

I've had fabulous luck in the Friends with Benefits (FWBs) category. It's the universe's way of karmically repaying me for my less-than-stellar luck in the Relationship category. Over the course of my life, I've had two long-term friends with benefits. From these men, I've learned some basic guidelines for a satisfactory FWB situation.

Rule #1: Proximity is key.

There needs to be easy accessibility the minute the horny bug hits. If you live in Manhattan and he lives in Brooklyn, it's never going to work. Like Sweet Georgia Brown said, "Ain't nobody got time fo' dat."

Rule #2: They can't be your real friend.

It never works when it's someone you hang out with on a regular basis in the daytime. Stuff gets complicated and it turns into that movie with Ashton Kutcher and Natalie Portman and then the EXACT same movie with Justin Timberlake and Mila Kunis. I reiterate, "Ain't nobody got time fo' dat."

Rule #3: Both parties need to be on the same page.

Clearly defined lines need to be established early on. You can't fall for your friend with benefits. You aren't dating. If either person finds a long-term commitment, the other person must gracefully accept this and fade out of that person's life and bed.

However, that doesn't mean either party has the right to be a totally inconsiderate asshole either. On the contrary, an ideal FWB situation involves some form of mutual respect. Otherwise, you'll hate yourself a little every time you call them.

I learned this lesson the hard way.

I met my first FWB, Joey, during my sophomore year of college. We went to high school together but didn't really know each other. He was a grade below me.

He was drunkenly stumbling down the hall of my dorm and asked for my AIM screen name. I was still reeling over the loss of Gustavo. Like any young, scorned lover, I was dealing with the heartbreak by consuming large quantities of alcohol and making out with anyone I could.

I did a lot of crazy shit that year in the name of loneliness.

Joey lived on the floor below me and was a giant asshole. Imagine the Tucker Max type: handsome, cocky, and a huge player. He was a ginger but the decent-looking kind, with no other outstanding features. He sent dick pics to random girls online. He was the kind of guy who wouldn't disclose if he had an STD. You know the type.

We hung out a few times and it became pretty clear that he was a major douchenozzle. At a different point in my life, I would have immediately said "C-ya!" But like I said, I was lonely and young. Plus, he lived super close. I didn't tell my friends that we were fooling around because I knew they would judge me, the same way I would have judged one of them if they had been hooking up with gingerdouchesupreme.

I was still a virgin, so when I say *hooking up*, I don't mean having sex. I don't even really mean oral sex. You're probably wondering, "What's left after eliminating sex and the exchange of oral pleasantries?" The answer is: you'd be surprised by how many ways you can get someone off. And no, I'm not talking about anal.[5]

Because I knew he was an asshole, I treated him like shit. I've never treated anyone else in my life that terribly. I'm embarrassed to admit it but a small part of me enjoyed it. He was friends with all the people who had made fun of me when I was a kid. He was part of the popular group, the kids who ruthlessly teased people who were different.

---

[5] Or the Mormon practice of floating, which involves insertion of the penis without any movement whatsoever.

I'm not proud of this, but I got off by putting him in his place, letting him know that he couldn't get everything he wanted. He liked it too. He told me that once. He said that for as long as he could remember, women had always been easy to get. He never had to work for anyone or anything. One time he complained, "All you ever do is take; you never give."

I thought about this for a second. He was right. I had the tendency to get off and leave.

"Then don't answer the phone when I call you," I said.

I hated myself a little for being such a bitch to him. But mostly I hated myself for being with him at all.

While we were hooking up, I found out that a casual friend thought she was monogamously dating him. She was still in high school and, in her own words, "falling in love with him."

"I think I've tamed the player," she told me. I had to break the news to her gently.

I immediately contacted Joey and told him I thought he was a terrible human being. He made a million excuses and rationalized while trying to get my sympathy. I cut him off and said, "You're making excuses and rationalizing and I don't feel sympathetic at all." I'm not sure why he cared so much about what I thought of him, but he sent a ridiculous number of AIM messages trying to win back my approval. He begged and promised he would change, to which I indifferently replied, "I don't really care what you do. I'm pretty over this whole thing."

He asked me if I hated him.

"I never really liked you," I said. "You treat people like shit and that makes you a shitty person." And to prove I meant it, I stopped fooling around with him from that day forward.

The good thing that came from Joey was that I learned what wasn't acceptable. I learned that there is a right way and a wrong way to treat people, even a friend with benefits. I learned that being horny and lonely is no excuse for feeding from the bottom of the barrel.

Luckily, after I graduated college, I met Tyler. He was awesome.

With Tyler I learned that FWBs don't have to be assholes. In fact, they don't have to come with the shame and guilt either. Some FWBs are amazing people.

The night I met Tyler, I was dressed like a robot. It wasn't Halloween. It was my friend Cici's robot-themed birthday party in July. Both Cici and I were quasi hipsters back before people hated hipsters. I loved beards and men in corduroy vests. Cici owned a lot of pleather and Goodwill shirts. The party was at one of our favorite bars downtown. I was dressed in all black with high leather boots, silver nail polish, and the creepiest looking full-face silver mask.

This was the summer of '09 and the *Twilight* craze was in full force. I spent a few Friday nights fantasizing about vampires and werewolves in my bathtub. When we arrived at the bar, my attention was immediately drawn to the boy who looked exactly like a blond version of Edward Cullen. He had the highest cheekbones I had ever seen and the fullest lips to match. Those were also some of the softest, most sensual lips I would ever kiss, but I didn't know that at the time. He was the most attractive man I had seen in a long time.

I had to have him.

So, while he was outside smoking, I was busy plotting ways to meet him.

I waited for him to return so I could make my move. I ambled over to the jukebox to choose a song for the birthday girl. After a long internal dialogue, I settled on "Total Eclipse of the Heart," when

Edward suddenly surfaced on my right to play a song as well. He looked over my shoulder, his eyes landing on my selection.

"Good choice," he said, smiling.

"Thanks," I said, smiling back.

We talked about music. (He liked Daft Punk.) We talked about our jobs. (He was trying to be a model.) We talked about our hobbies. (He liked biking and cooking.) We talked about school, our families, and everything in-between.

One thing became very clear, very fast: this kid was no smooth talker.

Through our conversation, I learned that he also used to be fat and his dad was a professional juggler. As a result, he spent the first fourteen years of his life traveling around the country and living with circus folk.

Maybe I needed to reconsider my dislike for carnies.

Since he didn't go to public school till he was fourteen, and when he did he was fat with long hair, he was pretty awkward to say the least. A formerly fat, awkward boy who looked like Edward Cullen? I was in love from the start.

Later that night he sent me texts about his neighbors having sex and how much it turned him on. For some people, that might have been a red flag. I found it arousing. We started out by having all-day texting conversations, usually with sexual undertones. Tyler's whole existence had a sensual undertone. I think it came from years of pent-up sexual frustration. Probably remnants of his fat-kid phase. I could relate.

A few nights later, we met at a bar, which was followed by an extremely passionate make-out session in my car.

Tyler and I spent a lot of time in my car that summer.

It was the summer after I'd graduated college. I had acquired twenty-five thousand dollars' worth of debt to get my degree and become a real, functioning citizen of society. Like most recent college grads, I was inadequately prepared for the "real world." I was broke, clueless, and had the same marketable skills as a fifth grader. So I did what every broke, clueless college grad does and ran full force, high-speed, right back home into the arms of my mother.

Living with my 'rents wasn't so bad. There was food in the fridge and heat I didn't have to pay for. However, there were obvious disadvantages. Namely my squeaky bed in a room adjacent to my parent's room. So, like my fifteen-year-old neighbors, I was fogging up car windows and straddling Tyler in the passenger seat.

My friends started calling Tyler "The Wizard" because he'd show up and I'd disappear. Also because he was so unnaturally pale that he seemed translucent. He was a wizard indeed, but his magic came in other ways if you know what I mean (insert Peter Griffin laugh here). He was passionate, sensual, kind, interesting, interested in my pleasure, and generally a great guy. He studied female pleasure spots by reading books on the *Kama Sutra* and watching educational videos.

So naturally, I broke one of the main rules of FWBs and started falling for him.

We started holding hands, going on walks, and I was mistakenly trying to hang out with him during the day. By October, in my female brain, we were monogamously dating. But I had to be sure.

"What are we exactly? Are you my boyfriend?" I asked.

"Oh. I mean…I thought we were just having fun."

I considered his response carefully. I was having fun but I had also developed feelings for this boy.

He was content with being casual. I wanted to be in a relationship. I wanted to go to the movies with him and cuddle. A Friends with Benefits situation simply wasn't sufficient.

I ended things immediately.

I didn't see Tyler until seven months later when I broke up with a different boyfriend. Against the advice of my friends, I texted The Wiz and said, "I would kill to be kissing you right now."

He responded with "Hey, stranger. Me too." We followed that with a barrage of sexts: "If you were here I would totally..." Followed by, "Mmmm, sounds amazing. Then I would..."

A lot of people don't get the point of sexting. I love it.

After two months of sporadically sexting, we met at our usual parking lot.

He kissed me deeply and stroked my neck.

At this point in time, I STILL hadn't lost the V card.

Tyler never pressured me to have sex. He was perfectly content with whatever I was willing to give. And I was perfectly content with that situation.

We fooled around for a few hours in the parking lot as if no time had passed at all. This time I had learned my lesson; I wasn't going to try to date him. I was ok with just being physical. Mostly because an evening with Tyler often meant five orgasms.[6]

After this first reunion, we continued meeting up for four more years.

During this time, both he and I would date other people and lose contact until one day one of us would send a text "just to say hi." If

---

[6] Without sex.

we were both single, we'd meet up in the parking lot outside of a bar, or later, at his or my apartment.

Our meetings were so random that it was too hard to develop real feelings.

Around the third year, we hadn't fooled around in a while.

"Have you been tested lately?" I asked.

"Not recently."

"You should make that a priority, I'd love to see you," I said.

And he did. That week.

I was seriously impressed.

He was the most amazing FWB. Not only did we both get off, there was mutual respect and trust. It was the most perfectly perfect Friends with Benefits situation anyone could ask for.

"I Found It On Craigslist And It Paid Really Well…"

I've only ever been fired from one job. Luckily it was the worst job ever. It was the end of summer after my junior year of college. I had just returned from California, where I learned to surf, did yoga on the beach, and spent all my money doing it. I was starting my senior year with less money than a crack addict. All I had left was my SoCal tan and an August bank account statement that read $5.56.

I needed cash.

I scoured the Internet for a way to make a quick dime.

After perusing Craigslist for two hours, I came across a "gig" that was perfectly suited for me. They were looking for fresh new "talent."

It was a job for desperate people. People who were too broke to care about their pride.

But it paid twenty-five dollars an hour.

Without any hesitation, I responded to the ad. They replied five minutes later to tell me that I was hired.

Just like that, I sold my soul to the Devil and started my career as a children's mascot. It was a poor choice, but at the time it seemed too lucrative to pass up. I didn't consider the implications or the consequences.

In fact, I was excited.

Little did I know.

In the world of mascoting, being five feet one or under is the equivalent of being six feet seven in the world of basketball. It's a golden ticket to every kid's birthday party, local county fair, or anything else that involves cartoon characters. Since I was four feet eleven, I was guaranteed employment.

My first gig was an event sponsored by the local cable company at the public library, to get kids interested in reading. The situational irony was not lost on me.

I was playing a character from the popular cartoon network show *Foster's Home for Imaginary Friends*. My costume was a giant chode-shaped, electric-blue blob with stubby arms and no opposable fingers.

I was told to arrive thirty minutes early and wear comfortable workout clothes. I nervously, yet enthusiastically, exited the car and headed toward the library doors.

Walking up to the desk, I said, "Hi. I'm working at today's event." The librarian behind the counter eyed me critically.

She squinted and in a nasally voice said, "There's an event today?" She grabbed the library agenda. "Yes. You must be in the Rainbow Room. Third floor. Past the bathroom. Second door on your left." She turned to sort her books.

I entered the elevator already mentally spending the money I was about to make. I sauntered into the Rainbow Room. A petite woman with short, blond hair and a large smile greeted me.

"Hello, I'm Tanya," she said. "You must be Olive?"

I shook her hand and smiled.

"I'm the representative from the cable company. It's my job to ensure that the event goes smoothly today. I need you to sign a few forms," she said, handing me a stack of papers.

"This is Charlotte; she's your personal assistant for the day. She'll be in charge of making sure you get your breaks, helping you get in and out of costume, and ensuring that the kids stay calm."

Initially, when I found out that I had my very-own-just-for-me personal assistant, Charlotte, I felt low-grade famous. My ego swelled. I was filled with a new sense of responsibility. If they were going to give me my own personal assistant and treat me like a celebrity, I was going to be the best damn mascot they had ever seen.

Charlotte helped me get into the costume. I bobbed up and down with energy. As we headed toward the room with the kids, she pulled out *The Official Mascot Rule Guide*.

"Rule one: the Talent is not allowed to speak. That means no talking at all," she said in a no-nonsense tone. "This extends to noisemaking, grunting, and 'mm-hmms' as well. The character is meant to be seen, not heard."

Charlotte continued to address me in third person.

"Number two: it is imperative that the Talent remains in costume at all times in front of the children."[7]

Charlotte's Nazi-esque demeanor should have been a clear indication of what was to come. She tucked *The Mascot Rule Guide* back into her purse. I was certain she kept it in her glove box so she could reference it at any given time.

I should have run out the door. Instead, I sauntered into the room full of children.

Within the first fifteen minutes, I knew I was in serious trouble.

It must have been over a hundred degrees inside the costume. I was boiling alive in my polyester sauna. Sweat poured down my face and stung my eyes until I could only squint. The eyeholes became too foggy to see out of. I stumbled around the room, hoping I wouldn't crash into any children.

The entire costume was attached to a piece on my back. The strain of it began to weigh on my shoulders until I could no longer stand

---

[7] This rule even included bathrooms, where I was forced to keep the costume on until I was fully concealed by the stall walls.

straight. Like an old man with brittle bones, I hunched over in pain. At the end of the first thirty minutes, my T-shirt was clinging to my body, saturated with sweat. I prayed for my first break to come soon.

In the mascoting world, breaks last for an entire thirty minutes and occur once every hour. When I first heard this, I thought that was an incredible deal. Twenty-five dollars for only thirty minutes of actual work. I was delusional and ill informed. Imagine the worst day ever, multiply it by thirty, get divorced, run over a neighbor's cat, have explosive diarrhea at work, wind up dead in a ditch, and it won't even come remotely close to mascoting. For a delirious heat-induced moment, I believed I had died and gone to Hell.

Finally my break arrived. I trudged into the breakroom while Charlotte helped me remove my head. By then I realized that the REAL job of the assistant was to make sure that the "Talent" didn't pass out from heatstroke. Or sneak out the back door. I slumped into a chair and stayed there for the rest of the break. After twenty-five minutes, Charlotte (who I began to like less and less) reminded me that I only had five minutes left. She grabbed parts of my costume, ready to assist with the torture. "Please don't make me do it. Please make my costume explode," I silently pleaded with the universe.

"Ok, time's up. Put your head back on," said Charlotte.

Easy for her to say. She wasn't almost passing out from the smell of her own sweat. I nodded, not so stoically, and replaced the enormous head.

As the hours continued to wane, so did my tolerance. The library was located in a wealthy town with a lot of housewives and spoiled children who got away with everything. The kids threw large objects at me, insulted me, and punched me. One wiped Cheetos cheese all over my costume, while another used me as his personal tissue. The overwhelming impulse to hit them grew with each passing minute. I'm an easygoing person but add in hundred-degree heat and even Gandhi starts throwing punches. I might have reacted violently but I was too exhausted to do anything but feel miserable.

For the next four hours, I cursed the cable company, my life, and every living thing within a five-mile radius. At the lowest point of my day, I allowed the bottom of the costume to rest on the ground. I hugged my knees. I stayed in this position for three minutes until I felt a small child poke me.

"MOMMY! Why isn't it moving? I think it's dead," he screamed.

"It wishes it was," I thought.

I felt him kick me in my left side as I struggled to stand again.

At the end of the gig, my shoulders ached painfully. I couldn't walk. I stumbled to my car, utterly defeated, exhausted, soaking wet, and smelly. As I fumbled with my car keys, I promised myself that I would never mascot ever again.

I didn't hear from the mascoting company for a while. I figured I had gotten a bad review from Charlotte.

So I was surprised when they contacted me seven months after my initial gig, to play Dora the Explorer for a two-day event at a sports stadium.

Given my prior experience, my natural response was "Hellz no."

Or that would have been my response.

Had I not been poor again. And had they not offered me the same luscious twenty-five dollars an hour that had originally sucked me down the rabbit hole to Hell in the first place.

So instead, I said, "What time should I be there?"

A few days later, I began to panic. It was the middle of a record-hot summer. I envisioned myself passed out on field, dying of heatstroke. As the event drew closer, I was filled with genuine dread. I started having nightmares where children were throwing poison-filled hot dogs at me. I woke up covered in cold sweat, panting.

I needed to get out of the gig. I emailed a representative from the mascoting company:

From: Olive Persimmon

Sent: Tuesday, July 15, 2008 11:45 AM

To: Mandy Falkenstein

Subject: Mascoting—Dora

Hi, Mandy!

I know it is short notice, but I was wondering if there is any possible way you can find someone else to cover this event? I'm worried that I may not be able to handle the heat. If you are unable to find anyone, I would be more than happy to do it.

Thanks!

Olive Persimmon

From: Mandy Falkenstein

Sent: Tuesday, July 15, 2008 11:49 AM

To: Olive Persimmon

Subject: RE: Mascoting—Dora

Olive: would prefer not to change now. Ok?

—Mandy

From: Olive Persimmon

Sent: Tuesday, July 15, 2008 1:43 PM

To: Mandy Falkenstein

Subject: RE: Mascoting—Dora

Mandy,

Absolutely understandable that you don't want to change. However, I would really appreciate it if you would try to find someone. I'll absolutely come through if you can't find anyone but I'm genuinely concerned that I'm not fit enough to be in the costume for that long without health repercussions. Would it be possible to call your other contacts in the area?

Thanks,

Olive Persimmon

From: Mandy Falkenstein

Sent: Wednesday, July 16, 2008 11:12 AM

To: Olive Persimmon

Subject: Mascoting—Dora: Cleveland Indians

This is to confirm that we are releasing you from the event in Cleveland as "Dora." Due to the high-profile nature of this event, we endeavored to staff it early on to avoid the necessity of trying to find Talent two weeks prior to the event. Sadly, this is what your email has required us to do. Thankfully we were able to find a veteran Talent from the Columbus area who is able to travel to Cleveland for the weekend. For your information, when we confirm you for an event we enter into a verbal contract with you and our clients. I regret to inform you that your service with us is no longer needed and your career as a mascot with this company is over.

Regards,

Mandy Falkenstein

I breathed a sigh of relief and congratulated myself for escaping. The money wasn't worth it. Mandy said it: my career as a mascot was over. It was the first time I'd ever been fired from any job, which was fine, because I'd rather be dead than mascot again.

PART 3: THE CELIBATE MOVES TO CLEVELAND

Somehow, The Celibate graduates college without having sex. She moves to Cleveland and hopes for better luck.

Cinco de Drinko

It was raining in Cleveland on the day I found myself at the public library checking out a book called *Fat, Broke & Lonely No More*. While everyone else had ninety-nine problems I really only had three, which happened to be the topics of this very book.

I imagine that most people see this book, skim through it, and promptly return it to the shelf. I took it home and actively hid it from my roommates. I read it in bed while eating Thin Mint Girl Scout cookies.

As part of a strategic life plan that I called "GET A BOYFRIEND, 2010," I was on my way to becoming rich, skinny, and taken. I started out by addressing the easiest variable to change: the fat problem. The gym became my second home. I knew all the trainers by name and always smiled at the other regulars. I was adamant about working out at least four times a week, for two hours each session. I ate protein bars and leafy greens and always did the appropriate amount of resistance and cardio.

Getting fit: check.

Rock-hard abs were in my future.

To fix the problem of being broke, I took a vow to stop buying shit that I didn't need. I took out some cash and rationed it into envelopes for the following weeks. I put my bank card into a small plastic container and placed the container in a bag full of water. I shoved the whole thing into the freezer, literally freezing my assets. Since I only had access to a small amount of money, I only spent it on things I really needed. Like food and Starbucks. I was no longer buying other "unnecessary" items, like haircuts and clothes. As a result, I was stuck with a ragged wardrobe, mustard-stained pants, and split ends.

In the name of saving money, I rationalized that it was ok to go to work with condiment-covered pants. One of my coworkers,

Meredith, saw the stain and gently offered me her Tide pen. Meredith always looked like she stepped out of a Ralph Lauren catalog. I laughed and said, "I'm always going to be the kid with some sort of stain on her pants. That's who I am! You know what? That's ok. I just have to get a job at a hot-dog stand." Though I looked a mess the whole time, I managed to save quite a bit of money with the freezing method.

Savings in the bank: check.

Unfortunately, while Fat and Broke were being addressed, Lonely was left unattended.

Rewind to three months before I checked out any book from the library. I had just moved to Cleveland, Ohio.

If I were a different person, this would be the perfect opportunity to take a cheap shot at Cleveland, but I'm not going to. I was born and raised in Ohio. If you ignore the eight months of crummy weather, the chronically embarrassing sports teams, and the complete lack of eligible bachelors, Cleveland is pretty great.

Moving is hard. Making friends in a new location is even harder. Without college classes and dorms, it's difficult to meet people in any new city. I moved to Cleveland for my first real nine-to-five job. I was the youngest person there and most of my coworkers were married with kids. While I loved all of them, the chances of them being my wingwomen at a bar at two a.m. were pretty slim. While college Friday nights were filled with booze and friends, postcollege Fridays in Cleveland consisted of watching *Gilmore Girls* and checking my phone for texts that never came. Needless to say, I spent a lot of nights feeling lonely.

Fortunately, though, I had an action plan to rectify the situation. It consisted of one simple step: make friends. Unfortunately, I never delved deeper than that into the plan.

I had a ton of friends, just not in Cleveland. I spent that entire first month hibernating inside and watching stupid TV shows. By the time spring arrived, I was stir-crazy and desperately in need of a social life. As the snow melted, my loneliness grew and eventually came to a climax on Cinco de Mayo. There's nothing like a Mexican holiday to make you acutely aware of all the fun you're not having.

I had just finished working out and was driving back to my apartment. I turned down my road when in my peripheral, I saw a group of college students stumbling out of a Mexican restaurant. They were obviously enjoying themselves. Suddenly I was struck with an overwhelming desire to partake in the festivities of the day. I imagined a fabulous evening where I was drinking margaritas and laughing over tacos. It was the perfect holiday to sit around and drink with the friends I didn't have. I decided that this was as good a time as any to execute my not-so-thought-out plan to make new friends. After all, there's no better way to get to know new people than copious amounts of holiday drinking.

I started out by sending a mass text to everyone I had ever met in Cleveland. The list included my trainer at the gym, my downstairs neighbors, a frat-boy friend of a friend, and Russell, a boy I had met at a bar once for twenty-two minutes.

I sat down on my kitchen floor, flipping my phone over every ten seconds to see if a text had come in. Nothing. I sighed deeply and decided to take a shower, get ready, and figure out a game plan. I didn't care who I was going out with but for damn sure I was going out with someone.

I got out of the shower and took my time getting ready. I dried my hair, slowly applied my makeup, got dressed, and headed back to the kitchen to check my phone. My heart fluttered in excitement when I saw the message icon in the corner.

"Love you. See you this weekend?"

It was a text from my mom.

I slumped back on the kitchen floor, totally disappointed. I flipped my phone a few times before having a revelation. Perhaps my texts weren't sending correctly.

"Hey, dude, text me when you get this," I sent to my best friend. She responded in less than thirty seconds with "got it." With no response from everyone else, I began to get a little desperate. My hair was done; my makeup was perfect. I was sitting on the floor in my kitchen all alone, eating string cheese. I kept staring at my phone, willing it to make any sign of life. With each string I tore off, I felt lonelier and lonelier.

I have this habit of unconsciously singing songs to reflect my mood. At that particular moment, I started slowly singing the lyrics, "I'm so lonely, I'm Mr. Lonely, I have nobody. For my own," in a falsetto, chipmunk voice.

After three minutes, I moved to drape myself dramatically across the top of two kitchen bar stools, my head and legs hanging off the ends. The volume continued to increase until I started belting out the lyrics.

"SOOOOO LONEEEEEELYYY. MRRRRRRRR. LOOOOONEEELY, I HAVE NOOOOOOOOOODDDY. FOR MY OWNNNNNNN."

Then in the height of my patheticness, when it couldn't get worse — it got worse. I sent the following text to everyone I'd previously sent a text to:

Me: "Hey! Be my friend in Cleveland, I don't have any and I need some. Soooo let's go celebrate Cinco de Mayo!! Margaritas and tacos! Woo-hoo!!"

(The text smelled of desperation, but I didn't care. Because at the time, I was feeling pretty desperate. Despite ignoring my original text, most of the recipients responded this time.)

Trainer: "Aren't you supposed to be on a strict diet plan? Margaritas won't give you that six-pack you keep talking about. Just go to the gym instead. See you on Thursday?"

Downstairs Neighbor: "Dude, is that you singing the 'I'm So Lonely' song?"

Me: "No, my roommate keeps playing it on her computer."

Downstairs Neighbor: "Uhh…yeah, kinda sounds like you."

Me: "Wanna go out for Cinco celebrations?"

Downstairs Neighbor: "Sorry, I have to work in the morning. Tell your roomie to turn down the music."

Frat boy: "Im alredy out wiht my bros, u should cum out! I didn't know u moved to CLE..Im wasssgssssted."

Me: "Yeah! I'm close your school, where are you guys?"

Frat boy: "We r on Coventry rd @ McNulsons..$2 drafts. Hell ya."

Me: "Cool! I'll be there in 20!"

Frat boy: "Uh yeah just talked to my bro, I think we r leaving soon. But— why don't you cum ovr to my house latr tonight ;)"

I waited thirty more minutes for some sort of affirmative response, with no result. My only hope was Russell, a boy I barely knew. No response.

It was pretty clear that no one was going to go out with me. After waffling for another ten minutes, I decided there was only one thing for a strong, independent woman to do: I lifted my chin, put on my stilettos, and decided to go out by myself.

I walked to a Mexican restaurant close to my house.

"How many?" the beautiful Latina hostess asked.

"Just one," I said confidently.

Instead of seeming impressed by my self-assurance and independence, she looked super annoyed and frantically looked around the restaurant.

"Um, would you mind sitting at the bar?" she asked.

"Sure, no problem. Just figured I might as well enjoy the holiday," I said smiling, trying to lighten her mood.

"Ok. Cool," she replied in a tone that made it clear that she didn't think it was cool at all.

She ushered me to my seat and gave me a menu. I ordered a margarita and a fajita, still patting myself on the back for going out alone.

I spotted two beautiful men across the bar. They were laughing a lot and flashing brilliant, white smiles. I waited until they glanced my way and flashed my best come-hither look. They sauntered over and both offered to buy me a drink. They laughed at my wit and humor, asked for my number, and playfully fought over it.

By that I mean, I smiled awkwardly at the old couple across the bar and made a lame joke to the bartender, who ignored me completely.

After exactly six minutes, it became painfully clear that going out by yourself totally sucks. Every few minutes I would look around, pretending I was really interested in everyone else's fun. I whipped out my cell phone and pretended to study it intently. I tried to give off the impression that I was an important businesswoman who had to go out alone because I was only in town for a few days for some conference. In reality, I was checking Facebook. By the time my food arrived, I was bored out of my mind and feeling super insecure about my eating-for-one status. I scarfed my food down as quickly as I could. I asked the bartender for a doggie bag and left my margarita half-full. I paid the check, threw some money down to tip, and hurried my ass out the door.

"Well, damn. That was a total fail," I thought while walking home.

I walked in the door humming the Lonely song under my breath. I cleaned off my perfect makeup, put on my pj's, and opened a

Corona. Despite just having eaten, I grabbed a bag of greasy chips and consumed them while watching *Gilmore Girls*.

By the end of summer, I had made a lot of friends in Cleveland. I had joined a few clubs and become friends with some young new employees at work. I returned *Fat, Broke & Lonely No More* to the public library. It was three months overdue. The fine was outrageous. The days of going out alone had come to an end.

Unfortunately, having a lot of friends meant that I was going out a lot. Which meant I was drinking more and spending a ton of money. I skipped gym workouts for happy hours and blew money on dresses to wear on dates. My thin-and-rich status quickly deteriorated.

But at least I had friends.

It was a trade-off. It all worked out because it's better to be broke, fat, and happy than thin, rich, and drinking margaritas alone.

Hot Dogs & Choking

Luke was the first guy I dated in Cleveland. I wanted to impress him. So I took him out for hot dogs.

Luke and I were both AmeriCorps VISTAs. We met at a training session. The first time we hung out, we talked about porn for a long time and wound up at a place called Granny's Cheese Palace (which sounds awesome but actually isn't).

Luke was handsome in an unconventional way. He was passionate about life and social issues. He wanted to change the world. He loved talking like a 1920s gangster and called everyone a "Cat." We quickly became friends.

"I wanna get sweet on you, doll," he texted me one night.

"I'm not exactly sure what that means?"

"It means I want to see you," he said.

My friend had just told me about a new spot called the Happy Dog. She raved about its menu of gourmet hot dogs. I'm still not convinced that hot dogs will ever be "gourmet" but this bar seemed to have found its niche. The toppings included things like escarole, "Everything Bagel" cream cheese, and bourbon pork-n-beans.

I loved trying new things and I knew Luke had a sense of adventure. I suggested that we meet at the Happy Dog.

When I arrived, Luke was already sitting at the bar.

"What can I get you, sugar?" he said.

I looked at the menu and decided to get a raspberry-truffle-mustard dog with Tator Tots and peas.

Luke ordered his dog and we started chatting. We were being flirtatious. There was obvious chemistry.

A few minutes later, some of Luke's friends coincidentally walked through the door.

"Oh snap," he said, waving at them. They headed over in our direction.

Our hot dogs came out at the same time his friends reached us. He introduced me, and then turned to catch up quickly.

While Luke was chatting with his friends, I went for my first bite of truffle dog.

In general, I eat too fast. I take giant bites that are too large for my mouth. That night was no exception. I bit in greedily, taking in far more than I could handle.

Before I knew it, I couldn't breathe.

It's impossible to describe the feeling of consciously knowing you aren't getting air into your lungs. Cognitively, it hits you that you're choking. When it does, the panic sets in.

I weighed the options in my mind. My first thought was to sneak off to the bathroom to try and rectify the problem. As I jumped off my chair, I saw visions of my lifeless body on the cold tile floor and reconsidered this option. This wasn't the time for pride. It was a good decision too because I found out later that the bathroom is the number one place where choking victims die.

I swallowed some beer to try and wash the dog down. It was unsuccessful. My lungs continued to become asphyxiated. After twenty seconds, I knew I needed help. I was going to die if I didn't get air soon. I turned to Luke, still in his conversation with his friend, and did some sort of choking gesture. He looked confused until he saw the panic on my face.

"Oh MY GOD! You're choking," he said.

As Luke slowly stumbled upon this revelation, I positioned myself over the bar and thrust against the edge in an attempt to "self-Heimlich."

The first try failed.

My desperation increased and I flung myself at the bar again. This time it worked. I projectile launched half-chewed hot dog and beer all over the bar and Luke's arm.

I gasped for air before looking up slowly to see the entire bar staring at me.

I was mortified.

I had two options: act awkwardly and make everyone feel embarrassed for me or laugh it off. I chose option two. Despite nearly dying a few moments before, I started laughing hysterically.

I hung around for a few more minutes, and then told Luke I had to get going.

"Are you sure, doll? We can go somewhere else," he said.

"Yeah, I'm not feeling too well," I said.

Luke sent me a few texts after that night but I was too embarrassed to see him. I had nearly died in front of him. From choking on a hot dog. I figured it was hard to make a comeback after that.

I thought the Happy Dog choking was an isolated incident. However, two weeks after that, I choked on a handful of almonds while driving. I choked again a few days later on a cookie. My new habit was causing me enormous amounts of eating anxiety. I was afraid that any bite could be my last. I decided I needed medical help. Concerned for my safety, I went to the doctor's office to address the issue.

"What seems to be the problem, dear?" my doctor asked in her nasally voice.

"I can't stop choking," I responded.

After a few tests and a lot of speculation (mostly on my part), my doctor diagnosed the problem. It was related to allergy sinus drainage and acid reflux. These two factors combined caused irritation and swelling in my throat, which made it harder to swallow food. Luckily, they were both problems that could be addressed. I breathed a sigh of relief, knowing that I wasn't destined for a life of choking fear.

Eight months later, I received a call from my friend Mary.

"Have you heard? Luke's been shot."

My heart stopped.

"What do you mean?" I said.

"Luke was shot yesterday. He's alive and at the Cleveland Clinic."

I called another mutual friend for more details. Luke had been shot in the throat in a drive-by shooting by his house in Cleveland. The man who shot him was on drugs and had never met Luke. Luke was alive but had trouble speaking since the bullet had penetrated his vocal chords.

When I first heard the news, I was shocked. He wasn't allowed to have nonfamilial visitors in the hospital so I waited on pins and needles to see him.

I rushed over to his house when he was finally home.

He looked normal except for a large bandage over his throat.

"Hey Cat," he said in a raspy whisper, standing up to hug me.

"Hey you. This is crazy," I said. It was the only thing I could think to say.

"I know. I'm just glad to be alive. They said my voice will probably return to normal in a year or so."

I hugged him, tears welling up in my eyes. We sat on the couch, no one saying anything for a few seconds.

"Don't cry. It's increased my street cred. I'm totally a badass now," he said playfully.

I laughed despite myself.

"How many people can say they've been shot?" he continued joking.

"Not many. Thank God," I said.

"You know, the last time I saw you, you were choking to death on a hot dog."

"I thought I was going to die," I said. I felt silly after I said it.

"See? Now we have that in common," he said, laughing.

"Were you afraid?" I asked quietly.

"Very," he responded in the same hushed tone.

I put my hand on his and hoped he felt reassured.

"You know what? I've lived in this neighborhood since I was a kid. I love it here. I'm not going to let fear take that from me. That's the thing about fear; it will consume you if you let it. I won't let it. I can't let it," he said more for himself than for me.

"You're very brave," I said.

He leaned forward. "You know, I thought it was pretty cool how you laughed it off after choking," he said.

I smiled. "This coming from a guy who just got shot."

"God. We're a pair of giant fucking messes." He laughed.

"But also badasses too," I said, high-fiving him.

"Hey. I never got to kiss you," he rasped.

"Can you?" I said.

"Don't see why not," he said, leaning in.

Then we made out, bandaged throat and all.

Groupon Glory

When Groupon first started, they launched an implausible, virtually impossible, publicity stunt where they hosted a contest for one person to live completely off Groupons for one year. At that point in my life, there was nothing I wanted to do more.

I had just started a new job. Like anyone starting a new job, I had absolutely no fucking idea what I was supposed to be doing at work or how to do it. Consequently, I spent a considerable amount of time pretending to work and trying to figure shit out. I also spent a lot of time looking for new apartments on Craigslist and shopping for coupons online.[8] In my diligent search for cheap stuff, I came across a new start-up company called Groupon. It was so new that they weren't even in Cleveland yet. I could sign up and be notified when they finally arrived.

A month later, Groupon rolled into Cleveland with the best half-price deals in town. It didn't take long for me to become a Groupon Junkie. Half-priced meals, half-priced shoes, half-priced adventures. I was in cheapskate Heaven.

This addiction led me to the "Live off Groupon" contest.

Keep in mind, this was before Groupon was a household name, before the infamous Super Bowl ad, before Andrew Mason was fired from the company. This was way before all that, before anyone even knew what Groupon really was.

The contest rules were simple: The winner would spend the year traveling around the United States with nothing but an unlimited supply of free Groupons. The winner had to start the contest in a paper suit made of daily printed deals. From there, they would need to barter, beg, trade, and strategize a way to get clothes and everything else they would need to survive. All without touching a

---

[8] At subsequent jobs, I discovered that most working people waste a lot of time doing this.

single dollar, dime, or penny. If after one year, the chosen person was able to live off Groupons, they won one hundred thousand dollars.

The chosen person needed to be resourceful, innovative, and insane.

I applied.

The application process involved posting two videos on YouTube and submitting an essay stating why I should be chosen. Instead of writing a typical essay, I figured I was better off with a question-and-answer format.

---

1. Who is this Olive Persimmon character?

Olive is just your average gal who used to look exactly like George Costanza and has unintentional run-ins with crack whores and circus folk. No joke, have you ever met one of those people that for some reason or another always find themselves in bizarre situations? That's me and my life.

2. Why should we pick her?

A. Sometimes I like talking in a robot voice to say things like "Total earthly domination begins now."

B. This is a shameless PR stunt by the Groupon staff, and I think that's awesome. So, you scratch my back and I'll scratch yours. (I mean literally...after all I have no money so all I can offer is a good back scratching. I'll even apply fake nails if you want.)

C. I'm a twenty-three-year-old Virgin. And no, I'm not ugly, smelly, or weird. (Possibly related to letter A ????)

3. What is Olive Persimmon greater than?

OP > Listening to "Total Eclipse of the Heart" on repeat.

OP > Realizing you can't actually get the clap from a toilet seat (and we all know there is no applause for the clap).

OP > Figuring out how to use the hashtag to solve your problems: @Kyleoppenhaur621-#Iwanttobreakup

4. Is it true that Olive B. Persimmon has a birthmark shaped exactly like Lady Gaga?

No, this is a blatant lie.

I submitted my application in Chiller font.

After a month or so of waiting and fanatically checking the Groupon website, the day finally came. Groupon was going to announce the seven finalists. Around three p.m., Twitter started going crazy with comments from other contestants. Everyone was lamenting receiving an email from Groupon letting them know that they wouldn't be continuing on in the contest. I was frantically checking my Gmail, searching for the same rejection email as everyone else. Nothing came. I started getting my hopes up. Around seven p.m., I checked my email on my smartphone in the craft aisle at Target. There was a personal email from Groupon's head of public relations. I guess the people at Groupon were fans of Chiller font because she let me know that I had been selected as one of seven finalists and only one of two females to move on.

I was going to fly out to Chicago for the next phase of the competition. I started jumping up and down.

I didn't have a ton of contact with Groupon after that until a few weeks later, when they emailed me to confirm my flight to Chicago. In an attempt to impress, I made a sequined shirt with a picture of Captain Planet on it. It read, "Groupon Is Greater than Captain Planet." I wore it over a paisley collared shirt. I remember thinking that I looked pretty cool. (Unfortunately, after I saw the footage from that day, I realized how insanely fat that outfit made me seem. I have a knack for making poor clothing choices.)

I was flying to Chicago and back in one day. Bursting with enthusiasm, I told the girl next to me on the plane about the contest. She gave me her number and told me to call her if I needed help navigating around Chicago. That set the tone for how helpful everyone was going to be throughout the day.

When I arrived at the airport, I had been instructed to find my driver. For the first (and probably last) time in my life, I found a man in a black suit holding a card with my name on it. As I entered the car, I was worried that there might be hidden cameras to see how I acted in real life. In hindsight, that's ridiculous. They weren't remotely organized enough to set up something like that. I made small talk with the driver and tried too hard to be funny (which always equates to not being funny at all). After thirty minutes, we arrived at the Groupon headquarters.

The head of public relations met me at the front. She greeted me warmly and made me sign a million papers before starting a tour of the office. I skimmed the documents but pretended to scrutinize them carefully. I wanted to give the perception that I was a responsible contestant.

The Groupon headquarters reflected the young CEO and staff. On each floor, everyone, including the CEO, Andrew Mason, sat together in one giant room. His desk was right in the middle of the other employees' with no outstanding features or markers. As we walked by, the entire staff started clapping and cheering, "George! George! George!" In my application, I'd told them about my middle-school nickname. It seemed they'd picked up on that the most.

Great.

Not only was I wearing an outfit that made me look super fat, they were chanting the childhood nickname I had when I was obese. Perfect setup for middle school flashbacks.

They showed me their Rock Band Room and Ping-Pong tables. They tried to show me their we're-a-successful-business-but-we're-so-cool-and-fun vibe. I was convinced. They were awesome and I totally appreciated it.

After the tour, they blindfolded me and guided me to a room with a video camera. An attractive, young hipster came in and interviewed me. He asked a bunch of rapid-fire questions. They weren't really interviewing me for interviewing's sake. They were doing it for a video compilation that they were going to use later to announce the winner. The entire video was regrettable, namely because it was the vehicle in which I discovered how fat a Captain Planet T-shirt over a button-down really makes you look. Damn, damn, damn.

After the video, they gave me three Chicago Groupons and told me I had exactly two hours to use them. I was instructed to be back at the Groupon headquarters at exactly four p.m. I would then write a blog post about my day.

I headed outside to some more "George" chants and started my *Amazing Race*–like adventure.

I ran out the door and asked a street vendor how to get to the Sears Tower. It was my first Groupon of the day.

"It's too far from here to walk, honey. You gotta jump on the subway to get there," he said, flipping some street meat.

My first obstacle. I had no money to buy a subway pass.

I headed toward the train and approached an older woman standing by the ticket machine.

"Hello, I'm in a contest to live off Groupons. I don't have any money…"

"Get a job," she muttered, cutting me off.

Wrong person. Wrong approach.

I saw a young couple enter the subway and decided I might have better luck with them.

I approached them with a large smile and immediately started explaining the contest.

"That's so cool!" the female said. "We'll buy you an all-day pass so you can use it to get anywhere."

I gratefully hugged them and continued my trek toward the Sears Tower.

When I arrived, I was overwhelmed with gratitude for the opportunity to be there as a participant in the contest. My Groupon gave me access to the top and also a year's membership.

I made my way to the Skydeck. As I overlooked the gorgeous view, I smiled to myself and said a quick thanks for my good fortune. Despite my time limitations, I wanted to enjoy the moment and savor Chicago. I sat down for a few minutes and took some pictures.

After fifteen minutes, I knew I needed to continue on my way. Two hours was not a lot of time.

I left the Sears Tower and headed toward the destination of my next Groupon. It was a famous hot-dog joint. My phone was low on battery so I had to rely on directions from strangers. Every few blocks, I'd stop and ask someone new.

On my way, I saw a bunch of young boys making a YouTube rap video. I told them about my adventure. They invited me to be a background dancer. They assured me that the video was going to go viral for sure. I shook my badonk-a-donk for several minutes until they got the shot right. I wished them luck and continued on my way to get some grubby hot dogs.

After several wrong directions, I wandered around Chicago, lost. Time was running out. I saw a mailman and asked him for directions. I was two blocks away. I ran toward the direction he pointed and finally found the famous restaurant.

I ordered two Chicago dogs. I looked at the tip jar with guilt.

"I'm sorry. I only have this Groupon," I said.

"Whatever. No prob," the teenage employee said.

After the great choking incident, I no longer ate hot dogs. I gave the dogs to a homeless man outside. He grumbled and told me he would have preferred a slice of pizza.

I wanted to use all three Groupons but I didn't have time. I had exactly seventeen minutes to make it back to the Groupon headquarters. I had no idea if there was a penalty for being late, but I didn't want to find out. I took off running. After five minutes, I realized that I had no idea where I was going. I stopped and asked a man at a newspaper stand. I was still pretty far away so I started sprinting again.

I arrived in front of the Groupon building with exactly four minutes to spare. I decided that the best use of this time was to get someone to buy me a brownie that I could give to the head of PR. Sucking up with food was always a good choice. I entered a bakeshop next door and offered to trade my final Groupon to a girl in line. She gave me a skeptical look and ignored me. I tried the guy behind her. He bought me a brownie with frosting. I handed him the Groupon for a discount mani/pedi and took off running back toward the building. I arrived exactly on time.

Sweaty and out of breath, I offered my brownie to the head of PR. She thanked me and told me that, oddly enough, three of the other contestants had brought food back for her as well.

Damn. I had some legit competition.

She ushered me toward the employee lunchroom. I had exactly thirty minutes to sit in the corner and write a blog post about my experiences. Employees popped in and out to grab refreshments and make small talk with me.

I scrunched my face up, reflecting on my day. Mostly it consisted of convincing people that I wasn't scamming them and begging them to help me out. I was selling them the adventure, telling them how cool the contest was and how cool they would be if they helped me.

I started my blog post with, "I woke up in the morning feeling like P. Diddy because I was a finalist in the 'Live off Groupon' contest." I figured a good pop-culture reference was a great way to start. I began writing about my flight to Chicago and my adventures at the Groupon headquarters.

After I'd spent ten minutes writing, Groupon's CEO, Andrew Mason, came in with a brown paper lunch bag.

"Oh, hey. Mind if I join you?" He said. He was wearing a faded Superman shirt.

My jaw dropped. The millionaire CEO of Groupon wanted to eat lunch with me. I mustered up my best smile and replied, "Of course!"

He sat down next to me and pulled a chocolate chip cookie out of his bag.

"This contest is pretty crazy, don't you think?" he asked, studying me.

"It's pretty exciting," I said.

"I mean, like, how would anyone even do it? What are you going to eat? You wake up in the morning and you want breakfast, and you only have Groupons. Isn't it going to be annoying to not be able to buy anything?" he asked. He was looking at me with intense curiosity.

"I'm super resourceful. I'd figure it out. I suppose I would just make sure I always saved leftovers. I'd look for Dunkin' Donuts trash cans where they throw out the day-old stuff," I said.

He looked disturbed. He asked me a few more questions about the contest and my creativity.

We chatted until his phone buzzed, presumably from the PR lady. He said, "Oh I guess my time is up. I'm supposed to let you finish your post. Nice meeting you." With that, he turned away and headed back to his desk.

I sat star struck for a few seconds, and then proceeded to write a decently-funny-but-not-hilarious blog post that detailed my adventures of the day. The PR lady hurried into the kitchen and gently nudged me to finish the post and pack up my stuff since the car to the airport was on its way. Surprised that there was no other formal interview process, I thanked her and said goodbye.

And then I waited.

And waited.

Two weeks turned into three weeks with no word from the people at Groupon. It was a bad sign. I emailed the PR lady to get back on her radar. She assured me that they were still making their decision and would let us know soon. Meanwhile, I spent most of my time daydreaming about my hundred-thousand-dollar life. I was mentally quitting my job and embarking on amazing adventures. I imagined a book deal and the prospect of becoming a low-grade celebrity.

I had become chummy with one of the other contestants, Josh. We had found each other on Facebook at the start of the contest and regularly chatted. We speculated daily about what was going on at Groupon HQ and shared our fantasies about winning the contest.

The day arrived. Groupon was going to announce the winner via a video on YouTube. I anxiously checked the website every three minutes, accomplishing nothing at my actual job. Finally the video was posted. It started by explaining the contest and showing all seven of the finalists. It went through clips of us all being blindfolded and interviewed. The final frame showed all seven of the contestants on the screen.

A giant X appeared on five of the contestants' faces, leaving only Josh and me remaining. I held my breath as the video stated, "And then there were two" in a dramatic voiceover.

It focused on the two of us for way longer than necessary.

A giant X popped over my face. The video zoomed in on Josh at the Groupon headquarters with everyone cheering.

My heart dropped. I shut down the video.

"Bye-bye, one hundred thousand dollars. There goes my fabulous life of being a D-grade celebrity," I thought weakly. I got up to grab a cup of coffee and drown my sorrows in an afternoon treat.

For months after that, people asked me about Groupon. I'd laugh awkwardly and tell them about my public loss. Three months later, everything finally died down and Groupon was fully out of my life. Or so I thought.

One day on Gchat, Josh messaged me and let me know that he was coming to Cleveland. He was a huge fan of Great Lakes beer and wanted to visit the brewery. After Cleveland, he needed to get to New York City to make an appearance on the *Today* show. I called my friends to see if they wanted to take a road trip to New York. They agreed. We offered Josh a ride to the city. We met him at a bar in Cleveland, and although he was jovial as always, seeing him caused me to have a revelation:

I had dodged a bullet.

Having no money totally sucks. Josh was forced to completely rely on the generosity of everyone else. He was wholly dependent on the hospitality of friends and strangers alike, often crashing on the floor in some random apartment belonging to people he had met that day. Although he had all the Groupons in the world to leverage, he had no money to pay for lodging, tips, or random hygiene products.

When we arrived in New York, we realized how difficult the challenge actually was. We had to pay for anything that Josh didn't have a Groupon for, which was basically everything. After purchasing his subway pass, dinner, and some other stuff, I was grateful that I had lost. In total, his expenses cost me over a hundred bucks. I was grateful that it wasn't me getting off a bus at six a.m. with nowhere to go and nothing to eat.

Though I would be lying if I said I wasn't jealous every time he appeared on TV. I eventually stopped following the contest. His blog was a little too detailed for someone of my attention span. It turned out that he made it through the entire challenge and did end up having some fucking awesome adventures.

He won the money.

I hope he does something cool with it.

Something cool like paying me back.

You're Dating a Virgin and Other "Oh Shit" Moments

I was physically, emotionally, and mentally ready to have sex. All I needed was someone to do it with. It was the first time I was Unintentionally Celibate.

I met Greg on the online dating site OkCupid. He was my ticket to sex. I just had to tell him that I was a virgin first. For most of the men I knew, dating a virgin was the ultimate dealbreaker.

Before Greg, I was the president and founding member of the Only Single Friend Left Club. While my coupled friends stayed in, I put on four-inch high heels in an attempt to find my next boyfriend. As a single lady, I participated in all the things that single ladies do: online dating, drunken bar-flirting, singing Beyoncé at the top of my lungs while shaking my hand like crazy. They all led to the same cycle of excitement and disappointment.

My life was full of casual relationships. One month here. Two weeks there. Half a day in '08. It was a problem because I wanted to have sex. But I didn't want to have casual sex. I wanted to have sex with my boyfriend. No man wants to commit to a relationship before doing the dirty. It was a conundrum indeed.

These casual flings never turned into serious relationships due to a multitude of dealbreakers. A dealbreaker is something so awful that it's impossible to continue dating, no matter how badly I wanted to have sex. There are many basic dealbreakers: bad breath, poor grooming habits, being rude to the waitress. The most common one is bad kissing.[9] If my partner couldn't meet my puckering standards, it was a total dealbreaker.

---

[9] When I first started kissing, at sixteen, I was worried about my skills. I watched countless videos on technique and read every *Cosmo* article on the Internet. I'd practice on my hand, perfecting my methods. I'd pucker wide and slip my thumb the tongue. I was practicing in my car once when a coworker rolled up next to me in her Subaru. I glanced over and it was clear that she had caught me. I avoided eye contact and peeled away as fast as I could. We never mentioned the incident.

Greg was an amazing kisser and didn't have any other noticeable dealbreakers. We started down the road to Boyfriend City.

There was only one remaining obstacle standing in the way of being a real couple. I had to get him to accept that I was still a virgin.

As a former twenty-four-year-old virgin, I speak with full authority on the topic. That's right, the big V. The unpopped cherry. The girl who puts the pussy on the pedestal. The chick who keeps her V card in a steel wallet locked up way down in Gringotts. No one was getting in but Harry Potter. I was an emaciated child in the third-world country of NoSex. I needed the Red Cross to deliver some Dick Aid.

I should have had sex in my car when I was sixteen like everyone else. Then it wouldn't have been such a big deal. But I didn't and time kept passing. Before I knew it, I woke up a twenty-four-year-old virgin. By then, being a virgin was an embarrassing dating flaw.

Plenty of guys said it wasn't a big deal. They pretended to be super cool about it.

But it was a big deal.

In fact, they would have preferred a girl with herpes; at least they knew they were getting some with that chick.

I met Greg after my twenty-fourth birthday. He was funny, handsome, and sensual. Sooner or later my virginity would have to come up. I thought about the best way to approach the subject. I'd had this conversation before and I knew there was a delicate way to handle things. After all, the reaction that follows the oh-shit-I'm-dating-a-virgin moment bizarrely resembles the cycle of grief.

Denial : "You're joking. Come on. You're fucking with me."

Anger: "Wait that can't be possible. Why are you a virgin?"

Bargaining: "But would you have sex? I mean if it isn't for religious reasons…"

Depression: "Shit, I wonder how many other guys thought they had a chance too."

Finally, they reach **Acceptance.**

Most men never made it to the acceptance phase. One guy stopped after anger and simply said, "I feel badly for you. You're depriving yourself of one of life's greatest pleasures for no reason." Given this reaction, I knew I carefully had to find a way to tell my new hottie.

I was dreading the conversation. Being a twenty-four-year-old virgin is uncommon. Every time I told someone, he immediately started trying very hard to figure out what was wrong with me. Did I have a third nipple? Was I crazy? Was I secretly a Mormon? I saw the wheels turning in their brains. They were frantically hoping that whatever freak-show oddity I was burdened with, it wasn't a dealbreaker.

Consequently, I spent a ton of time carefully crafting the perfect way to break it to Greg. I wanted to be smart about my delivery. After careful planning, I came up with this:

"Hey, babe. I have some good news and some bad news. The good news is that I have the tightest vagina you've had since you were sixteen."

I would pause after this line and let it sink in. I wanted it to become the consuming thought in his brain.

"The bad news is it's because I'm a virgin." I would quickly take a swig of my beer and then add, "It's no big deal."

I practiced a few times in the mirror and called Greg.

But even with practice, the best-laid plans turn to dust. When the subject came up, I was extremely awkward and stuttered for a minute before saying, "Uhhhh. Ummm. I have something to tell you."

"What is it, babe?"

Awkward silence.

"Soooooo...you're probably wondering why we haven't had sex yet..."

More silence.

"Hmmmmm...well...see...the...thing...is...umm...I'm...a virrrrgin...yep."

Any time I feel uncomfortable I elongate my words. So virgin lasted for at least ten seconds. My confession was followed by another painful silence.

"You there?" I asked nervously, holding my breath.

"Oh. You are?" he asked.

"Shit here it comes," I thought. "He's gonna get awkward and ask me why. He's going to ask a thousand questions. It's the beginning of the end." I was punching myself for not using my carefully crafted line. I hardened my heart, ready for another rejection.

"God, I'm so relieved," he said, letting his breath out. "I knew there was something going on but I figured it was herpes."

There you have it. I was wrong about the herpes thing.

We never ended up having sex though.

My virginity wasn't as much of a problem as his bleeding wallet.

I was his Sugar Mama. I frequently footed the bill for dinners and drinks.

He invited me to the movies once. We ordered our tickets from the teller and stood at the counter for an embarrassingly long time, neither party moving to grab their wallet. After what seemed like an eternity, I pulled out some cash and paid for both of us.

"Cool, thanks. I'll buy the snacks," he said, smiling at me.

At the snack counter, he commented on how expensive popcorn was and asked if I minded just splitting a small Coke.

The final straw came when he spent his last fifty dollars on a new piercing and was too broke to see me.

"Sorry. I just don't have any money for gas, babe."

My friends said it was an excuse. I had seen his ATM receipts. It was probably the truth. We broke up a few days later. My vagina was once again empty, alone, and unentered.

This meant I had another chance to use my perfectly crafted dialogue.

I practiced it again when I started dating Graham. I stressed and pulled my hair out thinking about telling him. As it turned out, he already knew. We were out at a bar one night when I said, "Hey, hon, I have something I need to tell you. Good news and bad news."

"Is it that you're a virgin?" Graham asked.

My mouth dropped open; I was dumbfounded. How did he know? Did my entire being scream virgin? Did everything I say allude to the fact that I had never experienced a penis in my vagina? My brain was running with a million different scenarios when he said, "Nick told me the first night I met you. He was like 'be careful with that one, she's a virgin.' Obviously I didn't care because I asked you out anyway."

And he didn't care. At least for a few months. That's a story for the next chapter.

PART 4: THE DEED GETS DONE

The Celibate has sex. Bow chicka wow wow.

The Eagle Has Landed

I wanted to have sex with Graham. Tons of sex. Coitus infinitus. Porn-star sex. In every room and in every position my overactive imagination could come up with.

When we first started dating, he seemed too good to be true. That's the way most relationships start. The beginning is always a honeymoon. It's all I-can't-keep-my-hands-off-you, let's-just-stay-in-my-friends-hate-hearing-about-you-naked-sext-pics-bullshit. That never lasts too long and things gradually start going downhill.

Then one day, the honeymoon ends. No more gushing. Silk undies turn into cotton grannies. Vaginal waxing is replaced by the occasional quickie razor trim.

There are always warning signs during the honeymoon phase that this is coming. But in the love-struck state, all red flags are ignored.

I should have been an expert in red flags thanks to ex-boyfriend Greg, but I wasn't. If I had been, I probably wouldn't have had sex with Graham.

My red-flag radar should have been so finely tuned that I should have walked away from Graham the moment I saw his perfect hair. Unfortunately, I was so thrilled that Graham was employed and paid for dates that I overlooked every warning sign.

And my vagina needed to feel what sex was like.

I met Graham through some mutual friends. He was the most conventionally attractive guy I've ever dated. He was a living, breathing Ken doll with a perfect six-pack. He was the former president of his fraternity and looked the part. The first time my female friends met him they commented that he was too hot for words. Truthfully, he was too hot for me. Way out of my league. He dressed in argyle sweaters and only wore sweatpants to bed. I wear sweatpants *to the mall*. He had slicked-back hair like a banker and used gel even if we stayed in to watch a movie. Also, he was mysteriously tan for it being February in Ohio.

On St. Patrick's Day, a drunk blonde came up to him while I was in the bathroom. She inquired with a disgusted look on her face, "Is *that* your girlfriend? She smells like pickles. You could do way better. Come talk to me and my friends."

Before the rumors start, let me clarify that I don't smell like pickles, at least not generally speaking. The point was that everyone could see that he was too hot for me. I'm no ugly duckling but he was model perfect and I'm more girl-next-door, first-grade-teacher cute. I'm the girl you introduce to your mom.

Graham was a very serious and rigid person. A man of routine. He ate chicken and broccoli every single night and laid out his clothes for the next day. He was high maintenance. The crowd he hung out with looked like they stepped out of a J. Crew ad. I'm more of an ad for "People of Wal-Mart." I'm perfectly ok with this.

He loved fancy nights out on his boat (yes, he had a boat) and wine tastings with the who's who. He was obsessed with maintaining his image. He had an incredible body and an impeccably clean apartment. He was perfectly charming when he needed to be. On our first date, we went to a Zagat-rated restaurant where you couldn't get a reservation for months. Graham's father knew the owner so we reserved a table with no problem. The food was delicious, but I felt underdressed.

As a solid member of the middle class, rich, insecure people make me feel awkward. Going to dinner with one is always the same routine. It starts with an uptight "posh" restaurant. They'll order something annoying with a hint of something else and a side of blah blah. The only way to fit in is to say stuffy things like, "Why yes, this wine does have woody undertones," when I don't know shit about wines and would prefer a beer. Then the waitress brings out a very, very small plate with a large amount of parsley and a small amount of food. The wealthy date will just rave about "the most (insert French word here) rack of lamb" they've ever had while I'm secretly using my phone underneath the table to Google said French word.

Rich, insecure people try to overcompensate by hiding behind fancy clothes and expensive adventures.[10] Graham was no exception.

I wasn't in love with Graham. I think I knew that we were never going to work long-term, but I was ready to have sex. When I was twenty, I wanted to have sex with someone I loved. At twenty-four, I wanted to have sex with someone who wouldn't give me an STD and would get breakfast with me in the morning. I needed to trust and respect them but I didn't need to love them.

I knew Graham respected me and he was clean. In my book, that was solid enough ground to do the deed. I was physically and emotionally ready to lose it.

After waiting almost a quarter of a century to let a penis enter my vagina, I had built up unrealistic expectations of how it was going to go down. I anticipated rose petals on the sheets and a passionate all-night romp. I imagined him carrying me into the room and caressing my face lovingly while Barry White played in the background.

But life's not a freaking Disney movie and truthfully it was anticlimactic. After heavy making out and fooling around he asked, "Maybe tonight's the night...?"

---

[10] The other annoying thing about wealthy people is their affinity for buying ugly lawn statues. Graham will probably have a yard full of eagles, gargoyles, and a cherubic angel pissing in a Koi pond. The only benefit to being a Lady of Leisure is that rich women get to wear enormous hats and no one calls them out for it. I hate pretentious wealthy people but I love hats.

I thought about it for a second and replied, "Yeah. Sure. Ok."

"You sure?" he asked, lighting a single candle on the bed stand and pulling out a condom.

"Yep. Let's do it," I said, kissing his arm.

And just like that, the deed was done.

He was gentle and overall the experience was A-OK.

When it was over, I commemorated by sending a mass text to all my friends that simply said, "The Eagle Has Landed." Everyone responded immediately with a barrage of OMGs and HOLY SHITs, and CALL MEs. The best response text was a combination of all of those: "SHIT. FUCK. OMG. OMG. WOW. FAAAAHHHK CALLLLLLLLLL ME."

After the initial elation of no longer being a virgin, things started going downhill with Graham. Not because of the sex, but because we were really different people.

The honeymoon was over. I realized he kind of sucked.

We started fighting regularly. He was weird about a lot of things. He made me feel insecure about wanting to have sex with him. I suggested that we try using costumes. He scoffed and said, "That's what couples do when the sex has become boring."

I tried to get him to shower with me. "Babe, that shower is too small for two people," he said.

Since I was new to having sex, he treated me like a child, often dismissing my ideas and belittling me. I suggested we watch porn together and he said, "Guys don't want to watch another dick while fooling around. Plus I don't like the idea of you thinking about someone else while we're having sex."

Despite the fact that he was my first lover, I knew there was something fucked-up about his ideas on sex. The last straw came one night when I was over at his house. I arrived and immediately started caressing his chest.

As I went to unbutton his shirt, he insisted he was too hungry and we had to eat first.

I understood. Sex takes energy and he had worked a long day.

After dinner, I made my second attempt.

He laughed. "Someone is feeling rowdy, huh?"

I nodded seductively and kissed him. As I started toying with his tie, he grabbed my hand and kissed it. "Babe, we gotta take Bailey out for a walk first. He's used to his evening routine."

I understood. Animals have needs too. It wasn't fair to ignore the dog because I was feeling frisky.

When we got back from the walk, I ran to the restroom to freshen up a little. I did a once-over of my vajay, double-checking for any lingering TP down there. I swished some mouthwash and walked out confidently.

Two steps out of the bathroom, I tripped on a cardboard box.

While I was in the bathroom, Graham had begun constructing his outdoor patio table.

I stared at him hammering and assembling.

It was that moment that I realized he didn't want to have sex. Graham loved doing things on his terms. He was an alpha male who needed to be in control at all times. He would only have sex when he wanted to. It didn't matter when I wanted to. I walked angrily to the couch and wrapped myself in a blanket.

"Hey, come cuddle," I tried.

"Sure, babe, one sec. I'm in the middle of putting this together."

Thirty minutes and an episode of *Golden Girls* later, I was still pouting on the couch, alone.

I tried to control it, but couldn't; I started crying. I knew he was going to think I was crazy and emotional but I didn't care. I felt wronged here.

Graham looked over and said, "You ok over there?"

I struggled to find the words and swallowed the lump in my throat. Through hot tears I said, "How do you think it makes me feel knowing that you would rather build a table than sleep with me?"

"Oh...sorry...I was just really excited about this table. I've been waiting three weeks for it to arrive." He came over and sat by me on the couch.

If looks could kill, I sent him one meant to take out an entire army. I struggled to find words.

Uncomfortable with the silence, he said, "If I can't satiate your sexual appetite, you can have sex with other men. After all, it's not like we're in a relationship." He made it seem like a joke, but it was clear there was some truth in there.

I was stunned. I stared at him in disbelief. If we weren't in a relationship, we were doing a pretty good job of faking it. Two days prior, I had spent the entire weekend with his whole family. Talk about sending mixed signals. I looked at him incredulously.

"Look, I mean, I'm just not ready to be in a relationship," he said with his own mixture of hurt and guilt.

Then the whole story came out. It was something he should have told me months before, something that would have explained so much about his behavior. It turned out that before dating (or not dating) me, Graham had a fiancée. She had cheated on him and he was pretty fucked-up over it.

Wow. Well that certainly explained his mood swings when that song "Jar of Hearts" came on.

There it was. I was more or less his rebound. I don't think he would ever classify me that way, but that's how it was.

Advice for the fellows: a recent ex-fiancée is information you should share.

Of course, there were warning signs that he had just come from a long-term relationship. Within the first month of dating, he bought me a hairdryer and shampoo for his house. By the second month, he bought me pajamas and invited me to fly home with him for his mom's birthday party. I was starved for attention and thought he was just being thoughtful.

I tried to be compassionate about his recent loss but the patio-table incident was too much. I didn't want to date someone who was emotionally and physically unavailable.

He left for a business trip to Boston a few days later. I decided to wait until he returned to terminate our relationship.

Except while he was gone, communication decreased dramatically. He was trying to break up with me first by pulling the old-fashioned fade-out.

Everyone knows, the minute you're ready to dump someone's sucky ass, when you've told all of your friends that you're "so over it," a strange phenomenon occurs. His calls start dwindling. He's "too busy to talk." Then you realize he thinks you suck a little too. You respond in the most unnatural way possible: by doubling your efforts to get him back. It makes no sense, but that's exactly what happened. How dare Graham jilt me when I was about to jilt him first? After all, I DID lose my virginity to him.

It was too late though. He had already decided that I was crazy. Ask any male about an ex and why she's an ex; he's 100 percent guaranteed to say, "She was cool until she went fucking crazy." Males absolve themselves of all responsibility.

So while I was trying to fix things with Graham, he was trying to distance himself from my crazy ass.

Upon his return from Boston, I didn't see him for a few days so I knew it was pretty much over. I asked him to meet me for coffee one night and he insisted he was "crazy busy with work." It was time to face the music. Needing closure, and with him leaving me no other alternative, I sent the following text: "Obviously this isn't working. Just wanted to let you know, no regrets."

Just like that, I text-message-broke-up with the boy I lost my virginity to.

Ok, technically he broke up with me first. Officially, I got the last word.

I never talked to him after that. My friends advised me to call him to get real closure. I'm not good with confrontation. I didn't know what I would say to him or what good would come from it anyway. I was too hurt and angry to deal with it. Instead I ignored it. In my mind, contacting him was weak. I couldn't let him see that he had hurt me. I turned my vulnerability into anger. I let myself be angry for a few weeks before I decided to take those angry emotions, put them in a box, metaphorically throw them in the river, and move the fuck on. Some call this tactic denial. I call it smart. At least smarter than sitting around for four months being depressed and eating ice cream all day.

I couldn't let the effects of Graham's robot behavior linger any longer.

"Every guy wants to watch porn with his girlfriend," I thought, shaking my head.

This was definitely a case of it's not me, it's you. I've found that humor is the best way to deal with hurtful situations. It took me awhile to fully reconcile everything that happened with Graham but once I did, I could finally see the humor in it. "What a strange, strange man," I'd say to my friends. To this day, when "Jar of Hearts" comes on, I shake my head and laugh a little.

The Gym Debacle

After my breakup with Graham, I hit the gym hard. There's no better revenge than looking and feeling great.

I loved my gym and spent hours there. That's why I was devastated when they asked me to leave.

I've been an avid gym-goer since the Costanza days. As a result, I've belonged to several gyms. Throughout my fitness journey, I've noticed some basic trends. Predominantly that gyms can be disgusting, germ-infested places. It takes a lot of time to find a good gym.

My first gym in Cleveland was trendy and expensive. It allowed its patrons to work out without socks or shoes. I complained once about it. The girl at the desk echoed my thoughts and said, "That's totally disgusting. I'm sure it's only one person that no one has caught." I let her know that it was, in fact, several patrons and a few trainers, so it really was an overall cultural problem. She promised that she would mention it to management. Two months later, nothing changed except my increased paranoia about contracting ringworm. After getting a bizarre rash on my arm, I decided it was time to leave that gym.

Quitting the gym is really an annoying ordeal. It's easier to get an illegal organ than quit the gym before the contract is up. I felt like I was breaking up with a clingy boyfriend. They asked a lot of uncomfortable questions.

"When did you see people without shoes? I've never seen that," the gym staff member asserted aggressively.

"It happens all the time," I stuttered.

My palms started getting sweaty as he studied me critically.

"Plus, I can't really afford it," I added to break the silence.

"What's your monthly gym allowance?"

"I can't afford any gym right now." My mouth started getting dry.

"Is there anything I can do to make you stay?" he asked.

"Look, I just don't think this is a right fit for me," I mumbled, nervously wringing my towel.

After I promised to sell my soul and get a note from my doctor, they finally released me from my gym contract.

I scoured the Internet for a new gym and came across one that was $12.99 a month. It was a deal I couldn't refuse. For being so cheap, it was a great gym. It housed quite a few cardio machines and a stretching area. I joined this gym six months before Graham entered my life. It was before I had friends in Cleveland, so I spent hours there watching TV and impressing the men with my knowledge of free-weight workouts.

Post-Graham, I spent even more time there. Exercise was a way to relieve my stress. I needed those endorphins. But truthfully, I just had too much free time. That's the worst thing about breaking up with someone—suddenly you lose your main activity partner.

Everything was going great at the gym.

Until a patron accused me of taping him on my cell phone.

I was on the elliptical watching a *CSI* episode and also sexting Tyler. I had contacted him a few weeks after the breakup for a much-needed self-esteem boost. In the midst of my sexting conversation, I became totally engrossed in the verdict being delivered on the crime show. I stopped pedaling and stared at the television screen. My forgotten phone hung haphazardly from my hand.

"She's taping me," I overheard a heavier gentleman telling his wife.

The comment barely registered. I was invested in the show.

"She's probably going to post it on YouTube," he said. His voice was becoming slightly agitated.

I turned slightly to see what he was making such a ruckus about. I noticed them glaring at me.

I looked at my forgotten phone. It was pointing directly at the man.

"We're all here for the same reason. You should be ashamed for making fun of me," he said.

Comprehension slowly sank in.

"Wait, are you talking about me? Noooo. I wasn't taping you. I'm just watching TV."

"Then why is your phone out," he spat. Smartphones were still relatively new. At that time, people weren't as addicted to their phones as they are now.

I hesitated for a minute. I couldn't tell him the truth. I couldn't say that I was multitasking by working out, watching TV, and sexting at the same time.

He took my hesitation as an admission of guilt. His wife snarled at me.

He walked over to the manager's desk.

The manager came over and asked to speak with me privately in his office.

"Have a seat." He gestured to a chair while closing the door behind him.

"We want this to be a supportive place where people feel safe," he said. He looked as uncomfortable as I felt.

"This is a huge misunderstanding." I was flustered. I couldn't believe what was happening. "I would NEVER do that. I was watching TV and using my phone to…"

I got stuck. The word *sext* was about to roll off my tongue.

"Um. I was just using my phone to text," I said.

Once again, my hesitation made me seem guilty.

The manager seemed uncertain about how to handle the situation.

"May I see your phone? If there's no video, then everything's fine."

That was a problem. Tyler had no idea about my current predicament. He was in the middle of sending graphic texts and pictures of his penis.

My face turned red. I felt like I was in the principal's office for a crime I didn't commit.

I loved this gym. I needed this gym.

But I couldn't let him see my phone.

"That's not going to be possible."

We were at an impasse.

"I'm really sorry but Ron's been a patron here for years. He was pretty adamant about his accusation."

"I can't show you my phone," I said.

"Well then…I have to believe Ron."

"We have a strict harassment policy here. I'm afraid I'm going to have to revoke your gym membership. You'll get a prorated refund for the rest of this month."

I stood silently in defeat. My phone dinged with a text message, presumably from Tyler.

That was my last gym in Cleveland. I didn't want to take the time to find another acceptable gym. I invested in some P90X DVDs instead.

The Winter of Earl

My decision to move to New York wasn't completely related to Earl Preezy. But he definitely had something to do with it.

Earl Preezy was the name of the crack addict in my basement. I only know his name and the fact that he was a crack addict because Officer Riley stated, "Sounds like Earl Preezy for sure. He's a crack addict." Later that week, my roommate and I would discuss banging Officer Riley. After all, there wasn't a ring on his finger. I digress. The real question is "Why was there a crack addict in your basement?" To which my response would be "How the fuck should I know?"

During the Winter of Earl, I lived on the border of East Cleveland. Despite its less-than-stellar reputation, Cleveland's a pretty legit city with some trendy neighborhoods.

Unfortunately, I couldn't afford to live in one of those neighborhoods.

Instead I lived on Belmar Road. Belmar is on the edge of cool. Two blocks to the right and you're in Coventry, the young hipster capital of Cleveland Heights. Coventry offers tons of cool college bars with beer-pong tables and hip restaurants that serve things like gourmet mac and cheese. Unfortunately, one block to the left and you're on Superior Hill, where the slogan is "Don't get shot after nine p.m."

That winter, I kept the local police in my speed dial. I called weekly. I've always been a frequent police caller. Some of it has to do with my overactive imagination, but mostly I consider it my civic duty. I'm a one-man neighborhood watch everywhere I go. Every time I see a weird-looking man with a small child, I linger and listen to their conversation just to be sure it's not a kidnapping. There was one time when it seemed a little too suspicious. I figured better safe than sorry, and reported it to the police. I never heard what happened. I like to think that I was the direct catalyst for a miracle where a small child was returned to her tragedy-struck family.

That winter on Belmar, I was genuinely afraid for my dysfunctional neighbors and their domestic disputes. Every night, I heard loud shouting and crashing objects. Right before the situation seemed to escalate out of control, I'd call the police and make them aware, just in case. I always imagined those TV interviews about some homicide where the reporter asks the neighbor, "Why didn't you do anything?" I never wanted to be the person who didn't have an answer. That winter, my downstairs neighbors were robbed twice.

The night Earl Preezy was caught lurking in my basement, I had just left to meet a friend when my roommate Jazmine called.

"Did you let a man into our basement?" she asked in a scared voice.

"What are you talking about?" I said.

"I went downstairs to do laundry," she said. "There was a man standing by the washing machine. He had no teeth. He looked insane and high. When he saw me he said, 'I live upstairs.'"

On Belmar, we lived in a house with three apartments, so we knew our neighbors. A sweet couple lived upstairs. Two college males lived downstairs. We lived in the middle. By default, the man without teeth did not live in our building.

"Why would I let someone into our house? What did you do?"

"I said 'Oh, ok,' and walked calmly up the steps until I was out of sight. Then I ran, slammed the door, locked it, and called you."

"WHAT! Did this just happen?"

"Three minutes ago."

"Have you called the cops yet?"

"No! I panicked and I called you first to see if you let him in."

I'm not sure why my roommate thought I would associate with a man without teeth who was obviously on drugs (let alone that I would let him into my home) but people think irrationally under duress.

"Oh shit! I just heard footsteps running up from the basement. I think he ran out the front door," she said.

"Hang up. I'm calling the cops. I'll be home in two minutes."

I called the police for the second time that week. In typical Cleveland Heights fashion, I received the goddamned answering machine. This wasn't the first or last time that happened. I hung up and dialed back. After three tries, I finally reached an operator. I told him to book it to Belmar.

Twelve minutes later, six police officers arrived at my house and headed down toward the basement. Our basement was the creepiest place I've ever known, even before Earl Preezy. It had a dirt floor and small rooms with doors made of broken wood. The lights cast dull shadows on all the nooks and crannies, which housed broken furniture and empty paint cans. It terrified me. When I did laundry, I bit my lip to prevent myself from screaming all the way up the stairs.

Officer Riley introduced himself first. He was young, handsome, and very concerned about our welfare. Jazmine replayed the entire scene of events while Officer Riley took notes. After a moment's pause, he identified our intruder as Earl. He didn't know why Preezy was in our basement but guessed, "He was probably just looking for spare change."

We looked at him, confused.

"To buy crack."

So Earl Preezy was hanging out in my basement to find spare change to buy crack. I didn't find that reassuring.

"He's a mean son of a bitch too," Officer Riley continued.

"Alright, there's not much we can do tonight. We'll go talk to Earl. Call the landlord and tell him you need a better lock. It seems like he walked right through that side door," another officer said.

I waited until all the officers left, and then called my friend Amanda. I was sleeping somewhere else that night.

I stayed with Amanda for three days, until I decided it was safe to go to my house.

I slept with the light on.

The next day I was walking to the grocery store when I heard a woman yell, "Hey, Earl. Come here and look at dis!"

I stopped breathing and quickened my pace. Was it the same Earl? Would he recognize me? Did he know we called the cops on him? I hid my face with my hand and turned the corner rapidly. I was living in a high state of fear.

Officer Riley contacted us a few days later to let us know that they had booked Earl for another unrelated charge. I was beyond relieved to hear that Earl Preezy wouldn't be lurking around anytime soon. Jail was probably the best place for mean men who break into people's homes to steal change.

Earl wasn't the main reason I decided to move to New York City. I wanted to be around the energy and creativity of New York. But Earl was a definitely a "con" on my pros-and-cons list for staying in Cleveland.

Sex Redemption

Tyler and I started texting a few weeks after my breakup with Graham but I didn't actually see him until a few months later. I told him about my awkward entrance into the world of sex. He was surprised that I was a virgin. I was surprised that after two and a half years of being Friends with Benefits, we'd never had that conversation.

"Weren't you curious why we never had sex?" I asked, shocked that he didn't know.

"I just assumed you only had sex with people you were seriously dating," he said sweetly.

He looked at me lustfully and leaned in to lick my ear. He whispered, "You know, if you're up for it, I would love to show you how good sex can be."

"Maybe," I said, seductively nibbling on his lower lip.

I wasn't sure I was up for it. I had just lost my virginity and I still wasn't interested in casual sex.

Then again, sex with Tyler wasn't really casual. I had actually known him way longer than Graham. Plus, we had incredible physical chemistry. I trusted him and he always treated me well. We had done almost everything but sex.

I wasn't ready to take the leap that night but I seriously considered his offer.

He invited me over a few months later. He was moving out of his apartment the following morning.

"We're not having sex," I asserted boldly via text.

I said it to set expectations. I wasn't certain that I meant it. I wanted to have sex with Tyler but I was still a little nervous after the debacle with Graham.

"I'm comfortable with whatever you want. Let's just see how your body feels and whatever happens, happens."

I knew how he made my body feel.

I was in trouble.

I walked in the door and was immediately greeted by some porn on TV involving a pregnant Asian woman.[11]

"What the fuck are you watching?" I said, laughing. He looked over at the screen and started laughing too.

"Oh, it's just a porn stream. All sorts of different things pop up."

I wasn't surprised that Tyler had a looping porn stream on his TV.

He came over, smiling, and started kissing my neck and my collarbone.

"Your skin tastes amazing," he said, trailing kisses down my shoulder.

I grinned, pleased by the compliment. I pulled his face toward mine and kissed him passionately on the lips.

Tyler always tasted like cigarettes and coffee. It was a taste I'd grown to appreciate and like.

He picked me up gently and started walking toward the couch. I wrapped my legs around his fit frame and started kissing his collarbone too.

After an hour of fooling around, I said, "Be gentle."

"Of course," he said, caressing my arm.

---

[11] Tyler and I both like Asians. It's my greatest dream to become a trendy Japanese break-dancer. I haven't figured out some of the key logistics yet but my dad always told me to dream big.

I won't go into detail about what happened next. After all, this is a classy book.

I will say that it was convenient that my feminist friend had given me three condoms she had acquired at a rally. I took them with the intention of using them on inanimate objects that I didn't want to clean after masturbating with. I never dreamed they would actually come in handy.

Afterward, we went to a twenty-four-hour grocery store. We bought some almonds, held hands, and kissed in the aisles. It felt really nice and couple-y. We headed back to his place and I slept while he spent the rest of the night furiously packing to move.

That was the last time I had sex.

If I had known I was going to enter a great sex famine for the next few years, I probably would have insisted we do it again in the morning.

That was August. A month later, I moved to New York City.

I saw Tyler when I came home for Christmas. We made out in my car for thirty minutes, until we saw a cop's headlights approaching. We laughed. It was just like the good ol' times.

Despite excellent physical chemistry, we really wouldn't be a good couple. On a lonely New York City night, I sent him a pathetic drunk text that lamented my loneliness and sadness. I immediately erased the text so I wouldn't have to remember it in the morning.

He responded with a dick pic.

It reaffirmed for me that he wasn't my boyfriend for a reason.

I haven't seen The Wiz for a long time, since he lives in Ohio and I live in New York. The last time I was home for the holidays, I was hoping he could break my sex rut.

I sent him a text. "Hey, I'm home."

"Hey! Glad to hear but I actually have a girlfriend."

So that was that. Someone else was enjoying the magic of The Wiz. I was mildly disappointed but still happy for him. He was a nice guy. He deserved to be with someone who made him happy.

And so do I.

PART 5: WAIT, ARE YOU FREAKING KIDDING ME?

There are only two chapters about having sex?

That's all the boning we're gonna get?!

Two measly, stinking chapters?

Yep.

You should have bought Fifty Shades of Grey instead.

PART 6: THE CELIBATE MOVES TO NEW YORK

The Celibate gets busy...but not having sex.

*And other stories that explain the kind of adult who becomes **Unintentionally Celibate**.*

Every Jackass's Secretary Gets Ready for Christmas

I was an Elf Entrepreneur. I was broke and my big plan was to sell singing telegrams dressed as Santa's little helper.

"We wish you a Merry Christmas and a Happy New Year," I sang in the shower in my best Chipmunk voice. My elf costume was laid out on the couch, my glitter eye shadow on the dresser, and my heart was full of heartwarming tunes that I could use to serenade my future clients.

I wasn't always willing to sell songs for money but I had been unemployed in New York City for months and I was desperate. I learned the hard way that moving to New York City isn't always Broadway and celebrities.

After two and a half years in Cleveland, I'd had enough. Some days I loved my job and some days I swore it was gonna give me an ulcer. I needed a change. I was tired of the gray clouds, the boarded-up houses, crack addicts in my basement, and my loveless dating life. Oddly enough, I adamantly defend Cleveland when an outsider says something negative. I can list over thirty famous celebrities from Ohio, cite the exact year that the Indians were in the World Series, and tell you that the hamburger and LCD originated there. Because even though it occasionally sucks, it's still my home.

But as much as Ohio was (and will ALWAYS be) first in my heart, it was time to move on. My friend, Cici had moved to Brooklyn, New York. After visiting her one weekend, I discovered that New York City was full of dreamers, performers, musicians, idealists, and weirdos.

I found my people.

I called up two of my friends and asked them if they wanted to move with me to New York, the city where dreams come true.

Or more realistically, the place where I'd be broke and living off three-dollar falafel from a street truck.

I recklessly moved to the Big Apple without a job or an apartment. My move was difficult because of the security I was leaving behind in Ohio. Specifically, a salaried job with health care and a spacious apartment with a fireplace. Type B personalities congratulated me on my sense of adventure and willingness to take risks. Type A personalities told me I was crazy and wished me luck in that sarcastic you're-really-gonna-need-it sort of way. Truthfully, the type A's might have been a little more on point. Plans are good. Plans would have prevented me from becoming insanely broke and spending every waking hour at Starbucks, stealing their free Wi-Fi and scrambling to figure shit out. Without plans, I cried on church steps and prayed for some job to come through while missing my fireplace.

I reiterate, plans are good.

My two roommates and I packed our entire lives into two suitcases per person and gave away everything else. We bought our red-eye bus tickets one week before we planned to leave. We woke up that morning excited and scared. At six thirty a.m., we hopped on a bus to begin the kind of journey that only young, naïve dreamers make. We arrived in NYC at eleven p.m., sweaty and stinking of recycled air. My best friend and her boyfriend were waiting to meet us. I couldn't stop grinning while taking everything in. I was in love with the lights and the chaos. We dropped our suitcases at her apartment and went to a trendy Mexican bar around the corner. While drinking an imported beer with my best friend, I thought, "This is the beginning of a really awesome adventure."

We started our apartment search the following morning. We began the search optimistically, Starbucks in hand. It quickly turned into a day from Hell. There's no language strong enough to describe the terrible process of finding an apartment in New York City. It's easier to fly to the moon than seamlessly get an apartment. We were working with an asshole broker we found on Craigslist. Before even seeing our first apartment, we had to get credit checks, show proof of income, let him talk with our guarantors, and promise our firstborn children. At that point, I wouldn't have been surprised if he had asked for blood and urine samples as well. After all that, he completely disregarded our space requests and budget, patronizingly saying, "Sorry, sweethearts, but you won't find an apartment in Manhattan for that price. Maybe in *Ohio*, but not here." One of the apartments he showed us was located directly above a well-known chain sandwich shop with a bizarre smell. Not only did the apartment have that weird sandwich odor, so did we when we left.

"Maybe we're being unrealistic about our expectations," I said to my roommates. "Maybe we have to live in a roach-infested apartment with no living room until we save more money."

Discouraged and disappointed, we met a different broker the next day. She was covered in tattoos and had dark-black hair. Her demeanor was casual and informal. That night, she helped us find our dream apartment. It had hardwood floors and brick walls, two things we never dreamed we would be able to afford in the city. Most important, it had a living room. Large living rooms in Manhattan are an extremely rare commodity. It didn't matter that we wouldn't be able to furnish it for four months; we were still proud.

The only downside was that it had two bedrooms. We had three people. This meant I was twenty-five and sharing a bunk bed. Over the course of that following year, every guy I dated asked, "How exactly does *that* work with a bunk bed?" I'd reply, "We'll figure it out."

"Good thing I have my own room," they all said, implying that there would be a safe place for sexy times. Sometimes though, it was too late to go back to my suitor's apartment—on those nights, we would cuddle in the bunk. It was then that I realized that there's nothing funnier than watching a grown-ass man climb your bunk ladder.

That was the beginning of my second dose of unintentional celibacy.

Our apartment was located on a corner with some conspicuous drug dealers but after living on the border of East Cleveland, I considered this an upgrade. It wasn't ideal for most people. For us, it was perfect.

Find an apartment: check.

Finding a job was a different story. I was completely delusional, believing my two years of experience qualified me for every awesome job on the planet. After submitting résumés for four months with no sort of response, I was deeply humbled and desperate for cash. New York job recruiters are reticent about hiring people FOB (Fresh off the Bus). I felt like I was thirteen again. I was broke, insecure, single, and trying to figure my life out. Unfortunately, the difference between twenty-six and thirteen is that in your teens it's ok to not have your shit together. At twenty-six, the lives of my peers were falling neatly into place. Every day someone on Facebook was getting married or engaged. LinkedIn informed me of everyone's fabulous promotions while Pinterest let me know all about the awesome baby shower ideas. It's a hard comparison for the rest of us muddling through our twenties and trying to land somewhere.

I was smack-dab in the middle of a quarter-life crisis.

My bank account plummeted, and at one of the lowest points in my life, reached rock bottom at $12.34. To conserve my precious resources, I started walking any distance below fifty blocks to save the $2.25 for a subway pass. Stereotypically, I was eating ramen once a day and perpetually on the prowl for free food. If the library was having an open house to celebrate its new computer lab and the flier mentioned appetizers, I was there. I became everyone's charity case. As my bank account declined, so did my self-esteem. I tried to keep a sense of humor, but even my sense of humor recognized that I was broke, and disappeared. Dating wasn't even remotely on my mind.

Although I was struggling, I couldn't let my friends in Ohio know how bad it was. My friends in New York understood. They had been there and had similar tales of couchless living rooms. It's a New York City rite of passage. It's a struggle that makes you hard yet grateful. It was too embarrassing to tell my former colleagues that I STILL hadn't found a job. I've never felt shittier in my life. One day, my former boss and mentor told me, "Honey, we're not judging you; you're the only one judging yourself. We have your back and we're proud of you." When I was feeling particularly depressed, I reminded myself of that.

Looking for a job became my full-time job. Suddenly everything in my life became a verb. I was spending five days a week "résumé-ing and cover letter–ing." Staring at the $12.34 number on my ATM receipt, I knew I was too broke to ignore it anymore. A friend suggested I contact the temp agency she used when she first moved to the city. Temping is a soul-sucking New York City ritual. Almost anyone who has ever moved to the city without a job has had to temp at one point in time or another. "New York City will kick your ass," my friend explained to me. "You have to fight for your right to stay here, and a lot of times that means you gotta start out temping or interning." I went into the interview at the temp agency in a full suit, with my briefcase from my previous employer. I could tell they were impressed.

"If I'm being honest, you're a different worker than we normally get," my interviewer explained.

"Where do you want to be placed?" he asked me kindly after a long conversation about my skills.

"At a nonprofit might be nice," I said. They called me the next day with a placement at a financial firm, the exact opposite of what I had requested. But beggars can't be choosers and when he told me the pay rate, I was sold.

I started the next week as a fill-in secretary for the general counsel at a huge investment firm. When I arrived, I was immediately thrown into the fire. Apparently, the temp company told the firm that I had several years of secretarial experience that I didn't have. Secretarial work isn't hard per se, but you'd be really fucking surprised how complicated a phone system can be. The guy I was working for wasn't a huge asshole, but he wasn't Mr. Rogers either. He was accustomed to his typical secretary, who knew exactly what he wanted for lunch and which toothpaste he used. He didn't know how to function without her. When he had to call in on an international conference call, he frantically came running to my desk screaming for me to connect him, which of course I had no fucking idea how to do. I walked out of the office feeling incompetent and inadequate. I called my dad, on the verge of tears, and he reassured, "It's only a week. You can do anything for a week." That became my mantra. "It's only a week. It's only a week." I repeated it fifty times a day.

The weirdest thing about temping is that it's a small glimpse into someone else's world. It's such a short amount of time, so no one wants to get to know you because they know you're already on the way out. It's like being the ugly stepchild.

Just like that, for the next several months I became every jackass's secretary. But it paid my rent and allowed me to live in NYC, and that was all that mattered.

While temping wasn't a high point in my life, it unfortunately wasn't the lowest point either. The low point came near Christmas, when I decided I needed extra cash for gifts.

After careful thought and consideration, I came up with the perfect solution.

I was going to deliver off-key singing telegrams dressed like an elf.

That's right. My million-dollar genius plan was to dress up like an elf and deliver singing telegrams. I would be lying if I said this was my original idea. I got it from my dad, who at one point in his life had an extremely successful singing-telegram business. And we wonder why I never turned out quite normal.

I already had the elf costume. My crafty roommate made one for me for SantaCon, an all-day binge-drinking festival to celebrate the start of the holiday season.

Costume: check.

All I needed now was customers. I rushed home excitedly after getting off the phone with my dad, my brain gushing with ideas. I opened my computer and created a flier. I used one of the pictures from SantaCon with my roommate and me in our elf costumes. I thoughtfully contemplated branding and marketing when coming up with my name and finally settled on Polly the Elf. Perfect. I created a new email account, PollyTheElf2012@gmail.com, and posted it on all my fliers.

After utilizing my basic graphic-design skills, I decided that the flier was just right. It was funny yet appealing. Colorful yet simple. I hurried over to the library to make twenty-five copies (that was all I could afford at the time). I canvassed my neighborhood, hanging them in the highest-traffic locations. I noticed that many of the poles where I put my fliers didn't have any other homemade advertisements. "Everyone must be too busy with the holidays," I thought.

Then I waited.

I checked my email every five minutes on my smartphone, a remnant from my old life. This continued for three days. Then one arrived. Ecstatic, I opened it.

It was from the city commissioner.

Dear Polly:

I am President of the 20th Precinct Community Council, which runs from 59th to 86th Streets. Although we realize your intentions are good, we write to inform you that the fliering ("postering") you are doing for your singing-telegram business is illegal, and carries stiff fines: $75 for the first flier, and $250 for each additional flier.

New York City Administrative Code Section 10-119 states, in part: "It shall be unlawful for any person to paste, post, paint, print, nail, or attach by any means whatsoever any printed material upon any tree, lamppost, telephone pole, public garbage bin, bus shelter, traffic-control device, or bench." This is a citywide law.

I grabbed a calculator and did the math: 75 + (24 x 250) equaled way more money than I had. In a complete and utter panic, I threw on my running shoes and sprinted out the door. I had no idea the next time the commissioner would be coming around but I wasn't taking any chances. Running as fast as I could, I ripped down every single sign on every single pole until I was certain that I had found all of them. Panting for breath, I headed home to think of a new way to make money for Christmas gifts.

I called my mom on the way home to relay to whole story. Big mistake. In the same way my dad's a crazy idea man, my mom's a practical realist. In the same way my dad thought my Polly the Elf singing-telegram business was brilliant, my mom thought it was the worst idea she had heard in the last ten years.

"Please tell me you're not serious. You didn't really post fliers to do that did you? It's dangerous! Do you really want to dress up like an elf and sing songs for a few bucks?"

I argued that she was being a little dramatic but it was a moot point because I had removed all the fliers anyway.

A few days later, I received an email from someone asking how much it cost for a singing-elf telegram. They must have taken down my email before I removed the fliers. My initial excitement about my business had quickly diminished after the email from the commissioner. Also, my mom's words had sunk in. I didn't really want to go to random apartments dressed like an elf.

In the midst of my fruitless job search—and unstable mental health condition thanks to temping—I didn't want to admit to another failure. I didn't have the balls to tell the soliciting customer that I was no longer in business. Instead I responded with most ridiculous and face-saving answer I could think of:

Thank you for contacting Polly the Elf for your upcoming holiday event. I appreciate your interest in my service but I regret to inform you that I am booked through the Christmas holiday season and no longer taking new clients. Happy Holidays!

Candy canes and mistletoe,

Polly

His Name Was Marlin Roberts

His name was Marlin Roberts.

For a dollar, he believed in me when I needed it the most.

I met Marlin in East Harlem. I was there by accident, courtesy of my terrible sense of direction. I was supposed to be at my apartment on the Upper West Side.

I was walking down the sidewalk, staring at my phone's navigation system, when a beautiful Mustang flew down the street. I was focused on trying to get unlost so I barely heard Marlin Roberts say, "Damn. What a beautiful car, huh, ma?"

Since I didn't realize he was talking to me, Marlin repeated, "Ain't never seen a car so nice, huh, ma?"

I turned toward the voice and noticed a broad-shouldered man in a puffy jacket a few feet away from me.

"Indeed," I replied, smiling slightly.

"You lost? Where you tryin' to go?" he asked, looking at my phone.

"Upper West Side. I think I got it."

"I'm heading that way too! I'll show you where to go," he said.

"That's ok, I think I'm good. Thanks though."

I increased my pace.

"Nah, let me show you. This is a bad area. These parts got dangerous people. Pretty girl like you, better to be cautious," he said, increasing his pace to match mine.

Those were my sentiments exactly. Especially with total strangers on the street. I became intensely aware of the lack of people around us. There wasn't a single other person in sight.

I reached in my purse and slyly grabbed my pepper spray. I slid it into my jacket pocket.

"Yeah, this is a dangerous area fo' sho. I'm only over here to get my papers," Marlin said. Before I could question which papers he was referring to, Marlin clarified that he meant his identity papers, which he didn't have because he had just finished a ten-year stint in prison.

Of course.

I have a natural talent for attracting people with "interesting backgrounds."

Marlin must have seen my worried expression. He said, "Don't worry now, ma! I'm harmless. I RESPECT women. I LOVE my mother. I would never hurt a woman." He stated it as if his personal testimony of himself would be sufficient to calm my nerves. He further vouched for his character by letting me know that he was only in prison for drug charges.

"I didn't hurt anybody, see," Marlin said, smiling with a toothy grin.

He tried to elicit my sympathy by telling me how he had lost everything: his fancy apartment, his cars, and all his women.

Throughout the tale, I was on high alert. As Marlin told me his entire life story, I walked rapidly toward a more populated road.

"He's gonna rape me and leave my body in the park," I thought, clenching my pepper spray.

"I'm Marlin Roberts. What's your name, beautiful?" Marlin asked with a twang.

"Rachel," I said, using my go-to name for situations that make me nervous.

"That's crazy!" Marlin Robbins exclaimed. "I had a dream about a Rachel just yesterday!"

"Oh did you?" I thought sarcastically.

As we reached the corner of Central Park, Marlin slowly reached into his pocket.

I knew that the game was about to change. I started breathing faster as the adrenaline raced throughout my body. My grip tightened around the pepper spray as I steeled myself to pull the trigger. Marlin turned to face me.

He said, "Rachel…I have to tell you, you have good karma. I felt it when you were walking by, singing. I thought to myself, 'Marlin, you must meet that girl.'"

"Oh God. Please let me live through this. I'm too young to die," I thought, holding my breath. I clenched my fist and inhaled deeply, forcing air into my lungs. My heart was palpitating, my mind racing. Fully expecting him to a pull a gun from his pocket, I was ready for action.

As I jerked my hand upward to pepper spray him, Marlin Robbins produced an item from his pocket.

It was a pack of tarot cards.

"Rachel! I want to read your tarot."

It took my mind a second to register what was going on. Once I did, I breathed a huge sigh of relief. I would live a little longer.

Although I was still afraid, my curiosity prevailed (as it often does). I had just moved to New York City. I was still temping and pretty depressed. I was desperate to hear some good news about my future. Maybe Marlin held all the answers I was looking for. Maybe he had been sent by the universe as a sign that I was going to be ok. He went from being a scary ex-con to a potential beacon of hope. It was irrational, but I let Marlin read my tarot.

The first card I drew, according to Marlin, displayed anxiety and fear. Marlin considered the card carefully. After a minute he said,

"Actually, this might be a reflection of how you're feeling right now talking to me."

"You need to calm down or I'll never get an accurate reading," Marlin asserted. I took in a few deep breaths and tried to calm myself, despite the fact that I was still talking to an ex-inmate.

Marlin spread the cards in his hand and told me to pick one that I felt good about. "Really feel the energy of the card, Rachel. Choose the one that connects with you the most."

I hesitated and hovered over one card for a minute, trying to "feel the energy" as I had been instructed. I paused and then quickly moved my hand to one at the other end of the deck.

Marlin stared hard at the card. I held my breath and prayed it wasn't the Death card or something equally as bad. After all, you become what you think you are. If Marlin told me I was about to die of cancer, I was really going to struggle to suppress that thought.

Marlin looked at me carefully and broke into a wide grin. "Rachel, something real good is gonna happen for you. You're gonna be real successful. Whatever it is that you're working on, it's gonna be good. Real, real great."

And you know what? When Marlin said it, I believed it. I was desperate for good news and here it came, for the first time in a few weeks, from ex-inmate Marlin Roberts. I looked at him gratefully and smiled. "Hey, thanks Marlin, I needed that," I said. I meant it too.

I turned to cross the street, when he said, "Uh hey, Rachel...I mean I hate to ask, but you know...times is hard. And well...I don't always read tarot for free, I mean you know..."

"Sure, Marlin, no problem," I said digging in my wallet for a dollar.

"Thanks, Rachel. I knew you was something special," he said as we continued to walk down the sidewalk.

We walked together for another block, chitchatting, until once again I remembered he was an ex-convict. Once again, I wanted him gone. My curiosity was gone and my fear resurfaced. We shared a nice moment. No point in ruining that. Now it was time for it to end. I told Marlin I was stopping in a pizza shop even though I had no intention of getting a slice.

"It was so great meeting you, Rachel. Maybe we should, you know, um…exchange numbers or something and we could hang out or something, you know."

"I'm not sure that's a great idea, Marlin. You're a really nice guy though and I wish you luck," I said kindly.

"Thanks, Rachel, you too."

Just like that, Marlin walked away into the sunset.

Until I saw him coming down the street two blocks up. Apparently I didn't wait long enough in the pizza shop. I quickly ducked into a bus stop sitting area and hid behind a poster for another five minutes until he passed.

I went home and told my roommates about my encounter with Marlin.

"Guys, I know we're feeling depressed about our current situation in New York, but I think everything is gonna work out. We're gonna be ok," I said.

"Of course we are. I tell you that every day," Mary said.

It was true. She was unfailingly optimistic. But apparently I needed an ex-convict to read my tarot to believe it. It was one of the best dollars I ever spent. So, thanks Marlin for believing in me when I didn't believe in myself. I hope things worked out for you too.

Finally "Make It"

After Christmas, I had a revelation. I needed to change my job strategy. Being conventional had never worked for me, yet I was trying to get a job in the most conventional way possible. I spent countless hours crafting thoughtful and well-written cover letters illuminating the skills I brought to the position. I researched hiring managers and personalized each letter with some tidbit about their college or hometown.

All this time, research, and energy amounted to absolutely nothing. It was time to change gears.

My aha moment came after a conversation with my bunkmate, Lindsay.[12]

"We need to change our attitudes," she said. "We've been sitting around all depressed and feeling bad about ourselves. We're never going to find a job that way. Our self-pity has a scent and everyone can smell it."

"You're right," I said.

"We can do this. We're smart, talented, and compassionate people. We just need to start being creative."

She was right. I was a creative person who was trying to be conventional and tediously normal. I took a sip from my mug and brainstormed. I could feel a well of mediocre ideas churning in my brain.

"I've got it!" I yelled, slamming my coffee on the table, spilling it everywhere.

"Magnets. That's the solution," I declared without a hint of irony.

"What are you talking about?" Lindsay asked, staring at me.

---

[12] In case you're wondering, I'm on the top. She's on the bottom. We both preferred it that way.

"I'm gonna start making magnets. From now on, I'm gonna go balls to the wall for each job I apply for. I have nothing to lose anymore."

I decided to test my new strategy on a nonprofit called Do Something. It was a young, trendy company. I desperately wanted to work for them. I read the bios of everyone on their staff, paying careful attention to their CEO. She was smart, accomplished, and young in spirit. Her bio highlighted the fact that she loved the term *amazeballs* and was obsessed with Justin Bieber.

I emailed my graphic designer friend Will. I asked him to design a single page filled with superhero speech bubbles, the ones that say "POW!" or "KABLAM" in old Batman comics. I requested that he fill the graphics with "Amazeballs!" and "Do Something," along with the traditional "Zap," "Blam," and "Kapow." He used bright, traditional comic-book colors. The result was perfect.

I took the graphics to work the next day, to my most recent temporary secretarial position, and cut them out secretly under my desk. I used foil and colored paper to make each magnet jazzy and flashy. The crafting perfectionist in me made sure each individual graphic was beautiful and unique.

My boss for that week walked by as I was gluing each graphic to a magnet. He looked at the magnets and back at me with confusion. But it was a Thursday, which meant that it was my second-to-last day at that firm until I was placed somewhere else. At that point, I was beyond caring.

When I was finished with the magnets, I constructed a list of the top ten reasons they should hire me. They were cheeky and included things like, "In addition to my ability to create and maintain relationships, I look pretty good in sequined headbands." There was a picture of Justin Bieber in the corner with a speech bubble that said, "Baby, baby, baby...just hire her." I meant business.

I placed both items carefully in a letter-size envelope with my cover letter and résumé behind it. I addressed the envelope directly to the CEO, crossed my fingers, and said a little prayer as I dropped it in the mailbox.

I received an email a few days later asking me to come in for an interview. I reread the email a few times and then shouted out loud in excitement.

"Thank you! Thank you! Thank you!" I exclaimed, expressing my gratitude to the universe.

I arrived to the interview ten minutes early, carrying a white vanilla cupcake covered in rainbow sprinkles. In my cover letter, I promised that not only was I a team player, I was the type of employee who showed up with a cupcake for someone's birthday. I was hoping someone was celebrating something that day.

I was sitting in the lobby when a young woman with strawberry blond hair came out to greet me. She was wearing jeans and a scarf. She looked like someone I'd be friends with.

"Hey, I'm Lisa. You'll be interviewing with me first," she said.

Lisa and I walked into a large, well-lit room, which was painted royal blue. Surfboards and other novelties hung on the wall. She thanked me for my cupcake and asked me some questions about the position and my personality in general. Things were going well.

For the next round, I'd be interviewing with Lisa, two additional employees, and the CEO, Nancy.

"Magnet Girl!" Nancy exclaimed when she walked in the room. She was confident and boisterous; her presence overshadowed everyone else in the room.

She sat down and made small talk, asking me where I was from and how I liked New York. When the niceties were done, she said,

"Ok, we're going to do a round of rapid-fire questioning. Just say the first thing that comes to your mind."

"Oh shit," I thought. I'm not good at that. I prefer to give thoughtful answers after I've objectively considered all facets of the questions.

"What's your favorite color?"

"Hmm…well I like a lot of colors, but I…"

"Just say one. It's rapid-fire. Don't think about it," Nancy said.

"Purple!"

"What song is on your iPod right now?"

"Billy Joel!" I said even though I didn't have an iPod and that wasn't an accurate answer. I was getting nervous.

"What's your favorite dessert?"

"Waffles and ice cream." This also wasn't true. At that point in time, I'd never eaten waffles and ice cream but there was a waffle truck outside and the woman eating waffles seemed to be enjoying herself. That's the fallacy with asking rapid-fire questions. The intent is to elicit the most-honest responses but I was just blurting things out.

"Which three causes do you feel the most passionate about?"

"Sex trafficking, education, and food-industry reform." These were accurate answers but not things that this nonprofit focused on specifically. I wanted the opportunity to explain why I felt so strongly about each subject. I wanted to clarify how I also supported the other causes that they worked for as well. That I believed, to the core of my bones, in ending homelessness and combating bullying.

But that's not how rapid-fire questions work because while I was trying to explain, she was already moving on to the next one.

"If you could meet anyone, who would it be?"

"Tyra Banks!"

"Why?"

I wasn't sure. I was shocked that answer had come out of my mouth. Three hours before my interview, I had been watching *The Tyra Banks Show* on TV when I turned to my roommate and said, "That woman is crazy. Look at her eyes!"

"Wouldn't you love to go to lunch with her?" my roommate responded. "She'd say the most insane things ever."

There I was, three hours later, in the middle of a huge job interview, stating that the ONE person in the world I wanted to meet was Tyra fucking Banks.

I was cracking under rapid-fire pressure.

"What's your favorite thing you've done in New York so far?"

"SantaCon."

Shit. I was a goner. I had just blurted out an all-day drinking festival with a bunch of wasted people dressed up like Santas.

I was mentally punching myself in the face for my response. It wasn't even remotely close to my favorite thing about New York. I loved the fresh farmers' markets every weekend and living in the same city as my best friend. I loved the chaos and energy. I didn't say any of this. I said something that made me seem like a slutty lush. I wasn't even a big drinker. I frequently went out and had one solitary beer. I could go for months without drinking. I wanted to explain that I only loved SantaCon because it was so uniquely the kind of thing that happens in New York. It was an opportunity for spontaneity and citywide interaction that I hadn't had in Cleveland.

This was going downhill fast. Nancy asked me a few more rapid-fire questions but there was no recovering from my last two answers.

Nancy stood up to leave. "I gotta run to a meeting, but it was nice meeting you," she said, walking out the door without shaking my hand.

The interview only lasted a few minutes longer. I thanked all my interviewers and walked out of the office, head in hands.

I stopped and bought a waffle with some ice cream. It was decent but definitely not my favorite dessert.

I'd blown it and it was a job I really, really wanted. I sat down on a park bench and spooned warm waffle into my mouth. "The universe always aligns the way it should," I reaffirmed for myself. "Everything works out as it should." I was resilient. I refused to go back in to my pre-Christmas state of depression.

While annoyed about the outcome of the interview, I was still feeling optimistic about my current life situation. I had another job interview later that week with a company voted the number one place to work in New York. My magnet strategy was working magic in ways I hadn't even dreamed of.

Before my next interview, I practiced answering rapid-fire questions with Lindsay. It was at another trendy, young corporation that provided free lunch every day. This time I showed up without a cupcake.

The interviewer was straight out of college and dressed in the fashion of the season. He was wearing a bow tie and skinny jeans. His hair was carefully combed to one side, highlighting his mastery of trendy hygiene.

His interviewing style was informal and casual, as if we were already great friends grabbing a drink. I hate this style of interviewing; it makes me too comfortable. It isn't smart to feel too comfortable in an interview because the truth is, he wasn't my friend. People go out and drink with their friends and get shit-faced and fall down in bushes. My friends are familiar with my mascara-stained face after crying for hours over a boy I just met. They've heard me fart, seen me vomit, and a whole slew of other gross things. These aren't things you want your interviewer to know about you.

Instead of asking normal questions, like "What skills will you bring to this position?" this hey-I'm-just-like-your-friends interviewer asked me to tell him a story. Just like that: "Tell me a story!" he said, crossing his legs and resting his chin on his hand.

I'm decent at telling stories so I obliged.

"Well, this one time, I accidentally picked up a man in a Statue of Liberty costume." I started weaving the tale. I'm not sure why I chose that one. Maybe I thought he'd appreciate the humor like most of my friends. About three minutes in, I saw by the look on his face that it was the wrong story to tell. I stuttered for a minute but it was too late. I was in the middle and I had to finish.

I learned a valuable lesson that day and it was this: If you're interviewing for a job and the interviewer asks you to tell him a story, it probably shouldn't be about the time you accidentally picked up a guy in the Statue of Liberty costume who legitimately turned out to be a stalker. We both laughed and he jokingly (but seriously) questioned my judgment.

I knew I wasn't going to get the job. "Shit," I muttered while walking out the front door.

I was fucking this up. And I was running out of magnets. I was a good employee and would make a great addition to any team. I just needed to convince everyone else.

I contacted a nonprofit recruiter to see if I would have any more luck with that strategy. I interviewed with her two days later. For the first time in weeks, I behaved normally in the interview. No cupcakes. No stalker stories. She seemed to like me and said she would call me if she had any opportunities available.

She called me a week later and wanted me to interview as a development associate at a nonprofit. I was thrilled. I was beyond exhausted by my mindless, boring secretary jobs. I felt like my brain was deteriorating into a mush of uselessness. I spent half of every day trying to entertain myself online. I would read the news in two languages, check Reddit, look up recipes for things I was never going to make, and apply to full-time jobs. All of this only took about four hours, which I meant I had four more hours of sheer and total boredom. At this point in the game, I was ready to accept any sort of job I could find.

The interview was scheduled for five p.m. I left my temp job an hour early to get down to the East Village in time. When I exited the subway, I was immediately enthralled with the location. I lived on the Upper West Side of Manhattan and didn't make it down to the East Village too frequently when I first moved. I was enchanted. It was a quintessential, artsy, quirky part of Manhattan. The streets were filled with students covered in tattoos and carrying musical instruments. There were cafés and specialty restaurants that only served pretzels or schnitzel. "I'd love to work in this area," I thought.

I walked down the street, inhaling the creativity before stopping in front of a church. I double-checked the address I'd scribbled on a piece of paper. It matched the black-plated address on the church. "Shit! I wrote down the wrong address," I thought in complete panic. As I frantically pulled up Google Maps on my phone, the door swung open. A polished older woman stepped out. "Olive?"

"Hello. Yes, I'm Olive. You must be Roseanne?" I said, extending my hand.

"I am indeed. Follow me inside."

I walked through the entrance of the church doors, past a large statue of the Virgin Mary and up a set of stairs.

"We rent the space on the second floor from the church," she said.

We walked into a large, well-lit room with pictures of Jesus on the wall. There was a Nativity scene on the table.

"We're a Jesuit organization," Roseanne said, noticing my prolonged gaze at the Nativity scene.

I had no idea what that meant except that it was a type of Catholicism, which I knew nothing about. I was raised by a Jewish mom and an agnostic dad without any heavy emphasis on religion. I was clueless when it came to organized religion. In fact, the last time I was at a Catholic wedding, I freaked out a little because I had no idea what to do when everyone got up for Communion.

Yet here I was in a church, sitting across from a Nativity scene, interviewing for a job with a Catholic nonprofit. Life is pretty funny sometimes.

Roseanne was not young or trendy. She didn't ask me to tell her a story or talk about my favorite dessert. I was relieved. I handled it better. The interview lasted three and a half hours. (That should have been my first indication of the inefficiency I was about to endure for the next year of my life.)

I had dinner plans at eight and inadvertently stood up my friend Kymian. She waited thirty minutes for me at the restaurant and after receiving no response to her texts (how could I call? I was in the middle of the interview) she left. I called immediately afterward and apologized profusely.

Roseanne emailed me two days later and offered me the job. I was ecstatic. I could finally utilize my brain again. I was going to be strategic and thoughtful. I could exercise my leadership skills and stop answering phones in my fake secretary voice.

It took seven months, but I had finally "made it" in New York City. I had a real job with benefits and a salary. I had my own desk again. I could make friends at work and truly help this nonprofit with my skills. My sense of purpose was renewed.

As it turned out, that year with that nonprofit was one of the most dysfunctional years of my life. (Seriously, when I think about it, I shudder.) "Making it" in New York City isn't always what it's cracked up to be.

But that was all in the future. When I saw Roseanne's email, I felt unimaginable joy and gratitude that I was employed. And I didn't do it with magnets or cupcakes. I did it with my good ol' fashioned personality.

Now that I finally had a job, I could focus on other things. Like dating maybe.

Two Titty Slappings, One Asian

When I first moved to New York, finding a job was my first and only priority. As a result, my love life took a huge hiatus. With it, my sex life as well. I dated a few guys casually but nothing that turned into anything. The New York City dating scene was unreliable.

I was visiting Ohio and hadn't had sex in over a year when my friend Mike Barlson said, "You should just have sex with Telmer."

Jacob Telmer and I had been friends since we were sixteen.

It's hard to describe him except to say that he laughs like a dolphin having sex and he's a very sweaty guy. For a while, he went through a tequila phase where he enjoyed getting naked and insisted everyone call him Tequila Telmer. Despite his outward charm and kindness, Telmer is the first person who told me about a disgusting sexual ritual involving frozen feces. It's called the Alaskan Pipeline. I strongly advise against Googling it; just know that it's repulsive and Jacob Telmer felt the need to tell me about it.

"You haven't had sex in forever. Telmer hasn't had physical contact in forever," Mike said, nudging me in the side.

"It makes sense," Barlson's girlfriend, Sandy, said.

"You and Telmer are exactly the same person. He's a weirdo. You're a weirdo," she said.

"I mean that in a good way, like, you're the fun ones," she added.

I needed a slumpbuster. Jacob Telmer was either the best solution ever or the worst mistake I could make.

There were some legitimately good reasons to have sex with Telmer.

He was hilarious, compassionate, and he always kept the fire going when we were camping. He was the life of every party and would frequently burst into the room with a crazy new story. He was inexplicably charming and awkward at the same time. We threw a roast in his honor for his twenty-fifth birthday. We all made sequined shirts with pictures of his face ironed on the front. That's how much we loved Telmer.

There were also three very good reasons why I should never have sex with Jacob Telmer.

He was Telmer.

He once mistook Blue Balls for testicular torsion.

He's been accidentally titty-slapped in his face twice.

Telmer spent most of his middle school career subconsciously avoiding girls. He was a late bloomer but ended up becoming the nerdy hot guy everyone wanted in high school. He never realized it though. By the time he started noticing boobs, everyone else was partaking in football-field orgies.

When Telmer turned sixteen, he started dating his first girlfriend, Lauren. She was five feet nine with mousy-looking hair. One night, after thirty minutes of heavily making out, Telmer decided to take the leap to touch his first breast. He nervously moved the tip of his finger under the edge of her shirt. Sensing no resistance, he inched his hand upward until it sat just below her left breast. As he was about to take the plunge and go for a fistful of glory, his good Christian girlfriend jumped up and decided it was time to go.

"I gotta finish my homework," she said, grabbing her purse.

"Sure. No prob. See you tomorrow?"

"Maybe," she said, quickly pecking him on the cheek before hurrying out the door.

As he watched his girlfriend leave, he noticed a throbbing pain in his groin. Telmer had never experienced Blue Balls before. He started getting nervous. His imagination ran wild as he imagined terrible things happening to his prized parts.

And he was sixteen. Sixteen for God's sake.

Certain that his dick was about to fall off, he went to find his mom. Telmer's mother was a nurse. She often diagnosed her unsuspecting children with uncommon illnesses. She was surrounded by horror stories all day and frequently assumed the worst.

After hearing the problem from her embarrassed son, she studied him carefully. Panic began to fill her loving face. Mrs. Telmer, unaware that Lauren had just left, declared, "Oh God. I think it's testicular torsion."

"Testicular torsion? Is it serious?" Telmer asked, his voice filled with terror.

"If we don't get you to a hospital immediately, you could lose a testicle," his mom said.

"Oh my God!" Telmer cried, his eyes wide with fear. In a tizzy, they ran around frantically, hell-bent on getting him to the hospital.

Curious about the commotion, Telmer's father walked into the kitchen. Both wife and son were running out the door.

"What's all the fuss about?" his father asked.

"Not now, Bob! Jacob is experiencing a pain *down there*. I'm worried it's testicular torsion," Telmer's mom explained hastily, heading toward the exit.

Comprehension passed over his father's face. "Didn't I just see your girlfriend leave?" he said.

Telmer nodded his head affirmatively.

"Why don't you try taking a cold shower, Son. If that doesn't work we will go to the hospital."

"This is serious, Bob! Don't you want grandchildren," his mother cried.

But Mr. Telmer was firm in his position.

Telmer stood in the shower, petrified that he was going to be the end of the Telmer dynasty.

The pain subsided. Telmer's treasures returned to normal.

He got out of the shower, slowly dressed, and went to the kitchen to find his mom. His mother was uncharacteristically avoiding eye contact. His dad asked, "Feeling better, Son?"

"Ya, I feel ok now but maybe we should have it checked out anyway," Telmer said.

"Son, I think we need to talk." His father chuckled, grabbing a beer and putting an arm around his son's shoulder.

Luckily, over the next few years, Telmer learned a little bit more about the birds and the bees.

But mostly he learned how to get titty-slapped by a woman.

Telmer's been titty-slapped twice. He wasn't expecting it either time.

The first time happened at a party being thrown by our friend's younger girlfriend. She was raging on Jell-O shots and Stoli. In her drunken state, her large breasts had begun to slide out of her tight tank top. Telmer entered the room.

Our drunken hostess squealed…

"TELLLLLLLLLLLLLLLLLLMMMMMMERRR!"

She ran over to hug him when one of her precariously placed boobs popped out and hit him in the face. Telmer yelled, "Whoa there!" while another party guest tactfully pulled up her shirt.

The second titty slapping is a little more epic. It happened in Canada.

With a stripper named Miko.

Telmer is a spontaneous dude. It wasn't surprising that on a boring Friday afternoon he called up Mike, to take a trip across the border. Before the new passport laws, Canada was the glorious land where underage kids from Ohio could drink and gamble before turning twenty-one. Beyond that and syrup, I can't tell you what Canada is good for. Telmer and Mike drove five hours to the Canadian playground. They were going to spend a few days in shady motels with fleas and get blasted for cheap.

Directly across from their motel was a skeevy strip club advertising "Hot Women" in neon lights.

"Shall we?" Mike asked, nodding in the direction of the sign.

"We shall, good sir!" Telmer said.

Mike and Telmer approached the strip club with the enthusiasm of most young boys and began to invest in the age-old art of drinking.

Also at the club on this particular evening was bachelor number one, Marty. According to Telmer, Marty was getting married for the third time and loved whiskey sours. He was wearing a cheap Hawaiian shirt. Marty was enjoying his "last night of freedom" by indulging in skanky women and well liquor. He was celebrating the evening with his two closest buds, who were fifty-five years old. None of them were wearing wedding bands. After a lot of liquor, Marty and company adopted Telmer and Mike into their bachelor party. With the wisdom of age, they began teaching the boys about one of life's finest luxuries.

Strippers.

Marty slung his arm drunkenly around Telmer's shoulder. He began to instruct Telmer about the lap dance.

"Ok, on the first song you're gonna pay her exactly ten dollars. No more. No less. She's gonna just take of her top, tease ya a little, you know."

"First dance, ten dollars," Telmer repeated.

"Second dance, you're gonna give her an additional eight dollars. Five makes you seem cheap and you can get away with eight so why waste two extra dollars? That will make her skirt come off," Marty said, nudging Telmer in the shoulder.

"Second dance, eight dollars. Got it."

"The last dance is crucial: you're gonna pay exactly twenty dollars. She's gonna get completely naked! Hello wet dreams, now don't fuck it up, kid. Do exactly what I said."

"Ten, eight, twenty. Ten, eight, twenty," Telmer recited, burning the dollar amounts into his memory.

Nervous at the prospect of receiving his first lap dance, he wiped the sweat from his brow. He walked slowly toward a room with red velvet curtains. He repeated Marty's instructions over and over in his head to ensure that he wouldn't "fuck it up" like Marty said. After parting the red curtains, Telmer was greeted by a chubby Asian girl dressed like a Catholic schoolgirl.

"You call me Miko," she said, grabbing Telmer by the hand.

She led him to a solitary chair in the middle of the room and walked over to a CD player in the corner. Miko turned on music, walked over to Telmer, and straddled him.

Telmer reached into his pocket with a sweaty fist and grabbed the crumpled-up ten-dollar bill.

Before the first line of the song was complete, Miko whipped off every last piece of clothing she had on her body.

Telmer, who had been repeating the three phases of the lap dance, was completely taken aback. Things weren't going according to plan. He got nervous. When he gets nervous, he laughs. It wasn't a subtle laugh; Telmer never laughs subtly. It was a full-throttle, high-pitched belly laugh that sounded like Minnie Mouse.

Miko stopped dancing. She folded her arms and pouted.

"WHY YOU LAUGHING??" she yelled angrily in a thick Asian accent.

Upon hearing this, Telmer lost control entirely and doubled over in his seat, his laughter shaking the entire chair.

Miko, feeling insulted, yelled again, "WHY YOU LAUGHING ASSHO!?!??"

As Telmer lost all ability to control himself, Miko's anger turned into rage. Without warning, Miko was up to bat. Her face contorted. She aimed, fired, and without any hand contact, used her left breast to smack Telmer in the face as hard as she could. The breast made direct contact and flung his glasses to the floor.

Telmer sat in shock, no longer laughing.

"You no laugh at me," Miko said, snarling as she walked away. Telmer sat silently in his chair for a minute, trying to figure out what had happened. As Miko exited the room, he crawled to the floor to find his glasses. After five minutes of searching, he located them in the corner. They were bent but intact. He put them on and slowly walked out of the red curtains.

"Why the fuck are you back so fast?" Marty hollered after Telmer emerged.

"She titty-slapped me," Telmer said, starting to laugh again.

"What the fuck do you mean? Sounds like it was going well then?"

"No, I mean, like, angrily titty-slapped me. Because I was laughing. She didn't follow the rules."

Telmer totally lost control and started laughing again, so hard that he couldn't speak.

"She didn't...follow the rules...ten, eight, twenty! I got nervous. So she titty-slapped me," he said between gasps of laughter.

After several minutes of confusion, Marty said, "Fuck her." He slung his arm around Telmer's shoulder. "Let's do shots?"

Mike and Telmer got so wasted that they didn't remember the rest of the evening. Apparently they tried one more time to get Telmer a lap dance but neither one can confirm if this happened or not. The only photo of the night shows them eating tacos. Telmer is wearing a woman's hat.

After telling us this story, Telmer said, "I want it to go on record, that just once...for the love of God, just once, I would like to be titty-slapped by someone attractive. Someone I'm actually trying to impress."

I wasn't sure I wanted to be the person doing it.

The Alaskan Pipeline, the testicular torsion, and the titty slappings weren't the main reasons why I couldn't have sex with Telmer. I couldn't have sex with him because...well...he was Telmer. We'd been friends for too long; it would be awkward and weird.

So, my vagina remained empty and Telmer's face remained unslapped.

A Woman on the Prowl

I wanted to make out with someone. An ex. A hot guy at the bar. I didn't care. I needed to feel lips on mine.

I had dated four or five guys since I'd moved to New York, but nothing that lasted longer than a month or two. Dating wasn't my first, second, or even tenth priority. It came behind my career, my friends, my public-speaking club, working out, writing this book, and pretty much everything else.

At first, I didn't even notice the lack of men in my life.

Then one Saturday night, after writing furiously for hours, I sat down on the train next to a handsome man. He had a neatly trimmed beard and smelled like cologne. I leaned closer to inhale more of his scent. The smell of Man drifted over my body, awakening long-forgotten urges.

The woman on the other side of him was overweight, which forced the two of us to sit closely. As his leg was squished next to mine, I started to feel the body heat emanating from both of us.

I'll be honest: it felt gooooooood.

Human contact is important. I had forgotten how amazing it felt to have sexual chemistry circling your body.

Everyone knows that it's proper train etiquette to move your leg when it's touching a stranger's leg.

I could have done that. Despite the lack of space, I could have shifted my leg slightly so it wasn't immediately next to his.

But I didn't. Because it had been a long time since I'd been touched by a man.

I savored the moment, reveling in the tension.

The bearded man exited the train at the next stop and winked at me on the way out.

Another handsome gent, this time a hipster who looked like he was from Brooklyn, sat down in the newly empty seat. As he sat, I carefully placed my leg so it would be touching his. I settled comfortably, waiting for the body heat.

After two stops, he stood up. Instead of exiting the train, he turned his back to me and awkwardly stood three feet away. He stayed there for another ten stops.

I stared at his back, laughing. Then I had a revelation: I had become the creepy person on the train.

Shit. Things had gotten bad.

In that moment, I made a decision. I needed to have physical contact with someone. Minimally, I needed a good make-out session.

That night, I texted some of my girls.

"We're going out tonight and I'm on the prowl."

I straightened my hair, put on a sexy dress, and was ready to find a prime make-out candidate. I ditched the granny panties that I had fallen back into the habit of wearing and put on some sexy undies.

I headed out with my roommates to meet our friend Kim at a bar she suggested. Kim was in a serious relationship. So I shouldn't have been surprised that our first bar was a classy wine joint. She'd been out of the dating world for too long. The only single men at a classy wine bar are there with their girlfriends.

After a couple of drinks, I insisted we leave.

We were on the Lower East Side, which meant that we were just a few blocks away from the famous Katz's deli.

I'm-in-a-relationship-and-I-don't-have-to-try Kim suggested that we go get pastrami sandwiches.

Wait. What? That's, like, the antithesis of making out with someone.

Then again, I did love Katz's. The Jewish side of me had trouble passing up a delicious kosher sandwich.

So I went. And I ate pastrami.

And then I smelled like meat and latkes.

Things were going downhill fast.

I sprayed perfume to cover the smell and inhaled some breath mints.

We left and headed toward the next bar.

We found a trendy one with a sign outside for picklebacks, Kim's favorite drink.

I immediately scanned the room for prospects, with the tenacity of a drunken frat boy. I saw a few lingering targets in the corners and decided the odds were looking better at this joint.

I put on my game face, squared my shoulders, and…sat at a table with my friends.

There were six of us, a few in relationships, so it made sense to get a table. In hindsight, no man wants to approach a table full of six women. Previously, I would have had no trouble approaching a man. This night though, I was out of practice. It was too bold of a move for someone who had been out of the game for so long.

We sat at our table and talked only to one another. We laughed and looked at pictures of someone's cat. I wish I were joking about that last part; I really do.

Toward the end of the evening, three members of our party left. Thirty seconds after they were gone, two males swooped in.

One of them was a cute teacher and he started chatting with me. Despite being cute, the effects of the alcohol were apparent. His eyes were squinty. He was slurring his words. As he put his hand on the small of my back, I should have been excited. Aesthetically, he was definitely make-out material.

But it was late and I was tired. The pastrami was not sitting well. Mostly, I wasn't sure I wanted to kiss someone who was that wasted. It was probably going to be sloppy and there was no flirtatious buildup.

"I think I'm gonna get going," I told the cute teacher.

"No, stay," he said, going in for a kiss.

I turned my head and he hit my ear.

"Nice meeting you," I said before turning toward my roommates.

"Time to go," I said, grabbing my coat.

Instead of making out with someone, I called it a night and went home.

And sat a little too close to a dude on the train.

Epilogue

I live in a city with 4,132,506 men and I haven't boned a single goddamn one of them.

I have a job, a steady income, and an active social life. I've learned how to intensely stare at nothing to avoid awkward eye contact on the subway. I'm a real, functioning citizen of society now. Unfortunately, I'm still Unintentionally Celibate.

Since I've moved here, I've casually dated an obscene number of professional musicians and finance guys in suits. I've dated men I met in the bar, friends of friends, and OkCupid matches.

I almost had sex with all of them.

Almost.

But not quite.

Sure, there were a lot of Big Apple orgasms, and occasional "just the tip–ing" but never full-on-p-in-the-v, pumping-hard-till-everyone-cums sex.

There were a million reasons: He didn't have a condom. I had a UTI. Jewish guilt. My period. I hadn't shaved that week. I have a bunk bed. His parents were in town. Second dates that never turned into third dates. Attempts at monogamous relationships that never turned into actual relationships. I was perpetually in a gray zone of "Is he my boyfriend? Should we have sex? What the fuck is going on here?"

None of them lasted long enough to figure it out.

As a result, I regret to inform you that I am still a Celibate. Not from lack of trying either. But I have a strategic plan and you're reading it. This book is my last-ditch effort before joining the nunnery.

Maybe some sexy single in New York City with a nicely trimmed beard and a good sense of humor will read this book. He'll be smart and educated (because he reads). Maybe he'll be a hottie from Brooklyn who found this book in a co-op sharing group.

Perhaps he'll find me funny or quirky. He'll take me on a date on the Upper West Side. Maybe that date will lead to another date.

That date will lead to some sensual, awesome boning.

Some sexy sex.

Some really intense and enjoyable coitus on a counter. Or in a Starbucks bathroom.

Maybe I'll even become his girlfriend and buy some racy lingerie to celebrate our four-month mark.

A girl can dream. Until then, you can find me in a café, writing about all the awesome sex I'm not having. I'll be wearing a hat and laughing to myself.

Acknowledgements

I'm lucky to be surrounded by people who vibrate on a different frequency and push me to be better and think bigger. Without them, this book would still be a few lonely essays on Google Docs.

I remember when I first told my mom about this book. I was terrified that she would be embarrassed of the tales I was telling.

"Stop worrying. We love you and we're proud of you," she said. That's the way it's always been. My mom has been my champion and advocate for years. She gave me approval when other moms might have succumbed to worry or fear. She loves and accepts me for who I am. That's the greatest gift anyone can ever ask for.

I want to thank my dad for teaching me that it's ok to be different. For encouraging me to think creatively. For telling me I could be anything and do anything I wanted. More than anything else, this mentality has shaped me into the person I am. Because of this, I've been able to accomplish more than I could ever have imagined. He also gave me the push I needed to finally finish this book.

Ian, you've been a steady rock for mom and accepted me as another daughter. I'm not sure what our family would do without you. Thank you for always slipping me a twenty when Mom wasn't looking. Mostly, I want to thank you both for always letting me have a place to sleep when I come home. For teaching me that home means a place filled with love.

Sis, thank you for offering to read and edit this book. For always being the first person to repost everything I do. For all the years when you bought more Christmas gifts than I did and still signed my name anyway.

Lexy, thanks for always waiting up for me until I got home. Between you and Bailey, you're the best dogs a girl could ask for. I hope there's double the amount of tennis balls in your next life.

Thank you to Nathan Wahl, who is a brilliant editor, a hilarious guy, and an amazing friend. He's the one who told me, "Speak your truth. Denial doesn't work in art." There's more talent in that man than a thousand other people combined. You should all hire him.

Thanks to Liz Byer for her meticulous copyediting. Her attention to detail is an art. You should all hire her.

Special thanks to J. L. and Katarina Kojic for allowing me to utilize their talents for the photos on the front and back covers of the book. Also to David Weinstein for designing the cover and making it look really freaking good. And for not getting annoyed with my constant emails about minor changes I wanted to make.

I want to thank the human resources team at CFC for being the first ones to tell me that I was funny. You know who you are. Also my friends at Humorous Toastmasters for reaffirming this message enough so I finally believed it.

Gratitude to my coach, Marina Romashko, for believing I could do big things. I remember when I was paralyzed by fear, you were the one who gave me the courage to move forward. Without you, I would have spent another four years editing. Also, thanks for always bringing the wine.

My roommates, Lindsay and Mary, for dealing with me when I was tired and hangry. For getting drunk and reading passages of this book to unsuspecting party guests. To Lisa, Krittika, Kat, Kymian, Leah, and Katie (and Fred) who read the entire book in its infancy without me even asking. For sending countless texts about how much they loved it. Your support always came in my moments of doubt.

I want to thank all the acquaintances and strangers who supported, shared, and liked my work on social media. You had no reason or incentive to love me but you did anyway. I hope you know that I love you too.

inally, I want to thank all my friends who encouraged and
ampioned this book. There are too many of you to name, and for
at, I'm beyond grateful. Sometimes I find myself wondering how
deserve to be friends with so many talented, enlightened,
ompassionate, ambitious, successful, loving, and kind people. You
ow who you are. Some of you have been my friend for over
en years. Some of you are newer friends. Regardless, your
port and love is everything. I'm lucky and grateful to have you
y life. I hope I'm half the friend to all of you that you are to me.
got your backs, always.

ce and Love.

P

Made in the USA
Charleston, SC
18 April 2015